Easy Dressmaking Techniques

Kathleen Blaxland

MILNER CRAFT SERIES

To my Grandmother

Angelina Descor Cole

whose dream I lived:

to teach others....

First published in 2001 by
Sally Milner Publishing Pty Ltd
PO Box 2104
Bowral NSW 2576
AUSTRALIA

© Kathleen Blaxland 2001

Design by Anna Warren, Warren Ventures, Sydney
Illustrations by Ken Gilroy
Edited by Donna Hennessey
Printed in Hong Kong
Photography by Cooks Hill Photography

National Library of Australia Cataloguing-in-Publication data:
Blaxland, Kathleen.
  Easy dressmaking techniques.

  ISBN 1 86351 281 0.

  1. Sewing. 2. Dressmaking. 3. Dressmaking - Patterns.
  I. Title (Series : Milner craft series).

646.4

Disclaimer

The information in this instruction book is presented in good faith. However, no warranty is
given, nor results guaranteed, nor is freedom from any patent to be inferred. Since we have
no control over the use of information contained in this book, the publisher and the author
disclaim liability for untoward results.

Contents

Introduction

This book is a guide to help all age groups learn to sew and understand the step by step instructions. If the samples are sewn in the order they are presented in the book and practised until they are fully understood, by the time you have worked through the book you should be able to make the garments shown in the photographs. The instructions are straightforward with easy steps to draft the patterns. It is an art to take a flat piece of material and make it into a convex shape to fit the body.

Sewing can be a wonderful hobby. You will also save a lot of money. You can even buy your own labels to give your garments that professional finish.

It might be that after a bit of practice and some success with your own garments you could start taking orders from friends. A few sales at a small profit would soon add up to quite bit of pocket money. Many famous couturiers have started out this way.

Good luck with your sewing days!

Sewing Kit

1. Sharp dressmaking scissors, to be used only on fabric, never on anything else.
2. Cheaper scissors for cutting patterns.
3. A tin of dressmaker's pins.
4. Tape measure.
5. Tailor's chalk to mark fabric.
6. Unpicker.
7. A packet of sewing needles in graded sizes.
8. A selection of cotton and polyester sewing threads. You must select the correct thread for a fabric to avoid sewing machine tension problems. The Needle and Thread chart on page 13 is very helpful.
9. Cheaper cottons can be used for tacking, provided they are the same colour as your garment.
10. Sewing basket to hold everything.
11. One yard (metre) of plain-coloured lawn to sew your samples.
12. Folder with clear plastic pages to hold you samples.
13. Small 5 ½ inch (12 cm) zip to sew your zip sample.
14. Thimble.

Sewing with a sewing machine

1. Have a clean neat area to work in.
2. Check your sewing machine is in good working order.
3. Put in a new sewing machine needle for each garment you sew, the correct size for the fabric you are using (see Needle and Thread Chart on page 13).
4. Use the correct thread for the fabric you are working with or the stitch will gather the fabric. Remember thread sews in a shade lighter than it appears on the reel, so choose colours carefully.
5. Make sure your scissors are sharp and only used for cutting material.
6. Have your pin tin handy; as you remove pins from the garment, place them in the tin.
7. Have your ironing board set up and test the fabric for the correct temperature. Always keep a press-cloth handy for fabrics that can't take direct heat.
8. It takes practice to sew a straight line. For practice, draw straight lines with a biro on some scrap fabric. Keep your eye on the needle and on the lines. Hold the material front and back to hep guide the stitching. Try not to go too fast-a steady even pace will give you the best results.

Sewing samples

Once you have mastered sewing straight lines with a sewing machine, it is very important to practice sewing samples. This will give you an awareness of the techniques and skills needed before you begin to sew a garment.

Keep your samples in a folder with clear plastic pages. Give each one a heading. You will find them a very helpful reference, the beginnings of the practical skills of sewing, and a way of learning the theory.

Remember, practice makes perfect.

Your sample folder should contain:

Stitched and turned seam	French seam
Run and fell seam	Neck facing
Binding a neckline	Making a rouleau
Darts	Waistband
Setting a zip	Slipstitching
Hand-sewn buttonholes	Machine-sewn buttonholes
Sewing on buttons	

1. Make small scale paper patterns of each sample first (7 inches/ 15 cm is a good length for seam samples).
2. You will need a 5 ½ inch (12 cm) zip for the zip sample.
3. A contrasting coloured fabric for the neck facing and neckline binding samples will help distinguish the parts. The plain coloured lawn fabric always represents the actual garment .
4. The waistband sample is cut to a 7 inch (18 cm length).
5. Iron the lawn before cutting out samples.
6. Keep making samples until you fully understand all the instruction. Keep the best ones for your sample book.
7. Decorate your sample book with cut-out pictures of garments from famous couturiers, or the couturiers themselves— a visual suggestion of a future career?

Pressing

Pressing your garment step-by-step as you sew will give professional results.

There is a difference between pressing and ironing:

Pressing is the process of lifting and lowering the iron. The combination of heat, weight and steam allows you to shape the garment as you sew.

Ironing is when the iron is pushed over the materials with a rotating movement, e.g. ironing a tablecloth or something flat.

1. Never press over pins, because they will leave marks in your fabric.
2. A covered shoulder pad is useful to hold under the garment in difficult curved or gathered areas.
3. Keep the press-cloth handy for fabrics that cannot take a direct iron, e.g. wool, velvet and some fine silks.
4. Before starting work on a new garment, test a sample piece of fabric to find the correct temperature.
5. A garment made in a heavier fabric, e.g. wool or taffeta, which you have pressed at each stage, will benefit from being professionally pressed at the drycleaners when it is finished. Label it clearly with a stitched on label, which says: 'New Garment, Press only, Please'.

Body measurement charts

Taking measurements

Ask someone else to take your measurements so they will be accurate. It's almost impossible to measure yourself.

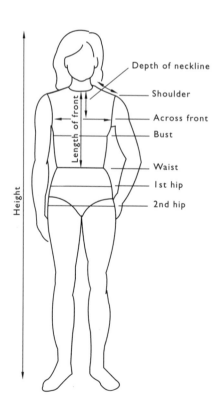

WAIST

Tie a cord around the waist to find its exact position. If making a skirt to be worn with a blouse tucked in, allow extra on this measurement for comfort.

BUST

Measure around the fullest part of the bust.

LENGTH FRONT

Measure from the highest point of the shoulder, over the bust and down to the waist.

LENGTH BACK

From centre back neck down to waist.

ACROSS FRONT

Measure from armhole to armhole, at the highest point of the bust.

ACROSS BACK

Measure from armhole to armhole, one-quarter of the way down from the nape of neck to the waistline.

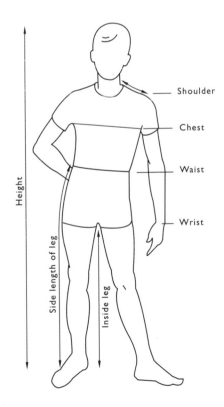

Boys

1ST HIP AREA
Measure around the hip, 4 inches (10 cm) below the waistline.

2ND HIP AREA
Measure around largest part of the hip, usually 8 inches (20.5 cm) below first hip measurement.

SHOULDER
Taken from neck edge to shoulder bone.

LENGTH OF ARM
Bend elbow, run tape from shoulder edge around elbow and down to wrist.

WAIST TO CROTCH
Sit on a flat chair with back straight. Measure from waist to seat; allow 1 ½ inches (3–4 cm) for comfort.

SIDE LENGTH OF LEG
From waist to floor; allow for hem and seams.

INSIDE LEG
From crotch to floor; allow for hem and seams.

Needle and thread chart

Fabric weight	Threads	Machine needle size
Very light: Georgette, organza, lingerie fabrics, heirloom sewing	Cotton-covered polyester—extra fine	60-70
Light: Handkerchief linen, lawn, paper taffeta, lace	Cotton-covered polyester	70
Medium Light: Gingham, satin, sheeting	Cotton-covered polyester	70-80
Medium: Flannel, corduroy, linen, velvet, poplin, shantung	Cotton-covered polyester	70-90
Medium Heavy: Denim, gabardine, felt, textured linen	100% polyester	90-100
Heavy: Corduroy, sailcloth, ticking	100% polyester heavy duty	100-110
Very Heavy: Canvas, upholstery fabrics	100% polyester heavy duty	110
Leathers and Vinyls: Leather, suedes, chamois	Spun polyester	90-100 Leather wedge point
Stretch materials: Knits, stretch velours	100% polyester	70-80 Ballpoint

Reading a pattern

Commercially produced sewing patterns have a picture of the garment printed on the front of the packet and on the back a description of the garment's sewing structure (or construction). If the pattern includes more than one garment, or more than one variation of the same garment, they are usually distinguished by labels such as A, B, C.

Size

Size is important. Make sure the pattern you choose is as close to your measurements as possible. Take time to study the pattern before you begin cutting out.

Cutting layout

The cutting layout shows the position of pattern pieces on the fabric; position will depend on your size and on the width of the material.

Selvedge

The selvedge of a fabric is the firmly woven edge on each side of a length of fabric. It is made during the weaving process on the loom. When cutting out a garment, remove selvedges to prevent puckering in the seam line.

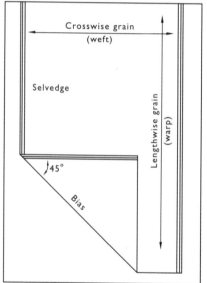

Direction arrows

Fabric can run three ways in a garment. The pattern pieces carry long arrows which show you the way your material should be cut:

Lengthwise arrows are used where the grainline of the fabric runs parallel with the selvedge in the pattern piece. The thread in this direction is called the warp.

Arrows across the grainline (horizontal to the selvedge) indicate the pattern piece follows the crosswise thread called the weft.

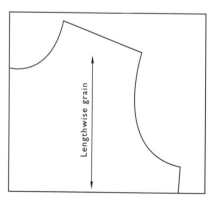

Diagonal (bias) arrows are used where the material is folded into a triangle on a 45° angle. The fold line shows where the stretch of the material is.

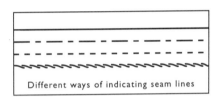

Crosswise grain

Cutting line

The heavy dark line marking your size.

Fold line

The marking where there is no seam line.

Seam line

The pattern shows a broken line.

Cutting line   Seam line   Fold line

Buttonhole position

Sometimes there is a separate strip of pattern with buttonhole markings which you lay on your garment to mark the distance between buttonholes.

Notches

Small V-shaped nicks for matching pattern pieces, which help keep the material on the correct grainline. Never cut too deeply into the seam line when cutting notches. (On sleeve pieces only, one notch indicates the front of a pattern piece; two notches the back.)

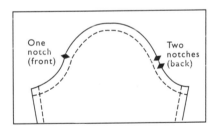

Different ways of indicating seam lines

Tailor Tacks

Thread markings indicating openings for zips, dart placements and other features which need marking once the pattern piece is removed from the cut fabric.

One notch (front)   Two notches (back)

Button position

A cross indicating where a button is to be sewn. Make sure it lines up with the buttonhole position.

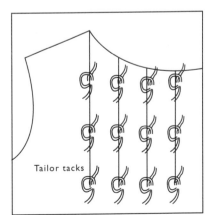

Tailor tacks

Pleat position

Arrows point in the direction the pleat has to be folded. Usually a fold follows an unbroken line marking going towards a broken line.

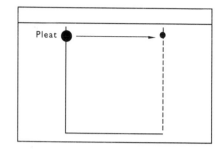

The toile

A toile is a calico 'practice' copy of the garment you intend to make. Using this you can perfect the pattern before cutting out your fabric. Darts and seam lines can be marked on the toile with biro to help give a correct fitting.

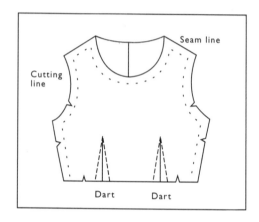

Cutting out

1. On the guide sheet supplied with the pattern, circle the correct pattern layout for your size and the width of your material.
2. Press the pattern pieces with a warm iron so they will lie flat.
3. Cut around the pattern pieces on the heavy black line. If more than one size is included on the pattern piece, pin through the pattern to the fabric on your size line. Lift the pattern slightly and mark at the pin line with tailor's chalk before cutting.
4. Make any necessary alterations to pattern pieces to suit your fitting. To shorten a piece, fold on adjustment line and pin. To lengthen, cut along the adjustment line and add a plain piece of paper the required length. Tape in place.
5. Press the fabric to remove any creases before pinning pattern pieces in place.
6. Use a pin to mark the right side of the fabric. This saves time when assembling the garment. The width of the fabric will determine which layout to use. Patterns have a 'Cutting Layout Shading Key' chart. Check this and follow as you pin the pattern pieces on the fabric.
7. Start placing the pins from the top of the pattern pieces and work

downwards, pressing any creases down towards the bottom as you continue pinning.

8. Transfer all tissue markings to fabric before removing pattern, eg: cutting notches, marking darts and circles with tailor's chalk

9. Keep one hand on the pattern pieces while cutting out. Keep material lying flat.

Tacking

Tacking is used when you start to join two pieces of material together. Tacking gives you a guide to match all your nicks and seams evenly. It also stops your material moving off the grainline. Use a single thread with a knot at the end, in the same colour as the fabric. Cheaper cottons can be used for tacking to cut cost.

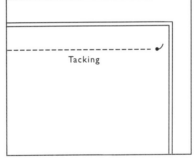

1. Sew ⅜ inch (1 cm) stitches evenly in and out of the fabric.

2. To remove tacking threads, cut individual stitches and pull out gently. Do not pull several stitches at once, or a very long thread, as this can cause puckering of the fabric.

Remember to pin straight, tack straight and sew straight.

Basting

Basting is a form of tacking used when you need to treat two layers of fabric as one so they will not move from the grainline. It is also used when interfacing is sewn into a garment. Thread a single thread, no knot. Make long slanting stitches 2 inches (5 cm) apart across the fabrics, taking care to keep the fabrics flat. Leave a tiny tail of cotton at the end of each line for removing the basting. Because these stitches are so much larger then tacking stitches they can be safely pulled out — but gently.

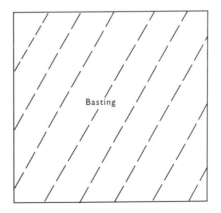

Tailor tacks

Tailor tacks are thread markings used instead of pins. They are very useful on patterned materials where pins might be difficult to see clearly, and also on sheer or delicate fabrics which pins can damage or slide out of easily.

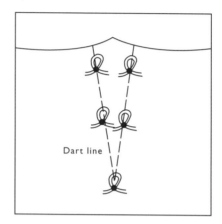

1. Use a double strand of coloured thread.
2. Sew a loop over the symbol you want to transfer.
3. Cut through the loop, remove the pattern tissue.

Seams

Stitched and turned seam

This is a neat tailored finish for light to medium weight fabrics. Even with the recent arrival of overlockers on the market for home sewers, the stitched and turned seam is still a very good neat finish. The trick is to get the right balance between thread tension and fabric weight. If the tension is wrong, puckering might appear along the seam. Work a test sample first.

1. With right sides of material facing together, pin, tack and machine along the seam line.
2. Press the seam open and flat; the two raw edges are folded down ¼ inch (6 mm) and machine-stitched close to the edge.

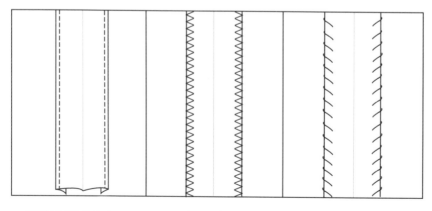

stitched and turned seam   zigzagged seam   overcast seam

Zigzagged seam

This machine finish is more suitable on heavier weight fabrics such as broadcloth and corduroy, and on some woollen-mixture fabrics.

1. Trim the seam allowance after machining the seam.
2. Change the machine needle to a heavy duty one; this will help the tension. Set stitch for medium width.
3. Turn knob for zigzagging and sew close to the edge.
4. You must have the right tension to prevent gathering.
5. Zigzag seams are practical for woollen of thicker fabrics, providing no stretching or gathering occurs.

Hand-sewn overcast seam

This finish will prevent fraying when sewing a very soft fabric, where machining and zigzag are not suitable and could cause puckering.

1. Press the seam flat open.
2. Thread a fine sewing needle with a single matching thread and a small knot at the end.
3. Starting at the top of the seam, sew diagonal stitches over the edge of the fabric, spacing the stitches evenly apart. Take care to catch the garment into the stitching.
4. Keep your stitches flat to prevent pulling.
5. Using a press-cloth and a warm iron, press seams flat.

French seam

French seams are suitable for both fine and sheer see-through fabrics. They look neat and prevent fraying. They are very practical for clothes which are laundered frequently, especially babywear and children's clothes.

1. Place wrong sides of fabric together (first stitching will be machined on the right side of the fabric.)
2. Pin, tack and machine a narrow ½ inch (13 mm) seam.
3. Trim evenly to ¼ inch (6 mm) wide.
4. Fold the seam over (roll the edge of the seam with your fingers) and press flat. Tack again just below the raw edges encased inside.
5. Check no threads are on view before machining.
6. Press the seam flat.

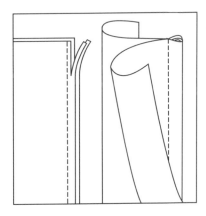

Run and fell seam (flat-felled)

This is a very sturdy external finish, very practical for sportswear, children's clothes and jeans. Using a contrasting colour thread can make a decorative finish, eg red cotton on navy material.

1, 2, 3. Start by following and machining steps 1, 2 and 3 as in the French seam instructions.

The next step constructs the run and fell seam:

4. The folded edge on the wrong side of the material is machined through to the right side of the garment, with matching or a contrasting colour thread.

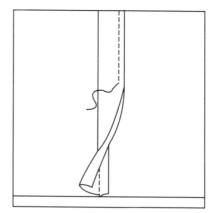

Hong Kong seam

Hong Kong seams have bias strips made from a soft fabric sewn to the edges. Matching ready-made bias binding can be used also. Very neat, this seam reduces bulk on woollen and heavier weight fabrics, and is very suitable for unlined garments.

1. Stitch seam and press seam flat open.
2. With right sides of bias binding and right side of seam edge, machine a ¼ inch (6 mm) seam.
3. Press fold over to the underside.
4. On the right side, stitch in the crevice of the fold.

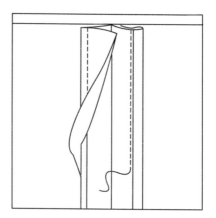

Facings

All facings on a garment, eg: neckline, front and back neck openings, must line up perfectly after being sewn to the garment. Any sign of pulling or puckering means the garment will lose its professional finish. Match all nicks and symbols, always tack in place, be careful not to stretch.

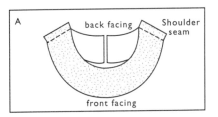

1. Join the front and back facings rights sides together at the shoulder seams. Press the seams flat open.

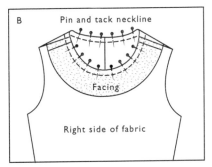

2. With right sides of facing and garment together and matching shoulder and neck seams, pin and tack around neckline.

3. Machine around neckline and remove tacking.

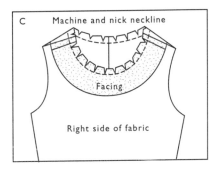

4. Trim the seam and nick it ¼ inch (6 mm) apart all around the neckline to help it to lie flat in the curved areas. Be careful not to cut too deeply towards the stitching line (Fig C).

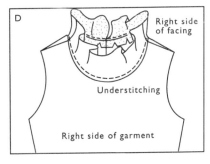

5. Turn facing to the inside of the garment, roll the seams with your fingers and press flat.

6. Understitch the seam allowance to the facing (Fig D).

7. Neaten the raw edges of the facing by turning and machining close to the edge.

8. Holding a shoulder pad underneath the facing, press it flat. This helps to prevent stitching the neckline.

9. On the wrong side of the garment, slipstitch the facing to the shoulder seams.

Interfacing

Interfacing is an extra layer of fabric which provides extra support, helps the shape and prevents stretching. The type of interfacing you choose depends on the garment fabric. Interfacing is available in light, medium and heavy grades, in both sew-in and iron-on types. The non-iron or sew-in interfacing is usually set into woollen or similar, heavier weight fabrics, the iron-on type being better for lightweight fabrics. Interfacing is used in collars, front or back openings, lapels, waistbands, pockets and some pocket flaps. Its use is illustrated on pages 31 and 35.

1. Always follow the pattern instructions for a particular garment.
2. If using the iron-on type, trim seam allowance before fusing to avoid unnecessary bulk.
3. Sew-in interfacing is basted in position to prevent it moving from the grainline. The garment section and the interfacing are then treated as one piece.

Understitching

Understitching keeps facings and seam lines from rolling to the right side of the garment. Always trim and remove any bulk from seam allowances before understitching.

1. To understitch a facing around the neckline of a garment, pull facing out flat and on the right side machine close to the seam line and through the seam allowance underneath. This stitch is not visible on the main part of the garment.
2. When understitching collars, cut the seam allowance along edge to eliminate bulk. Turn the collars inside out and, as far as possible, understitch on the wrong side of the collar.
3. Side pockets in skirts or frocks will stop pulling out if a row of understitching is machined as far

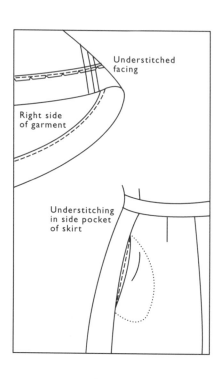

Understitched facing

Right side of garment

Understitching in side pocket of skirt

down on the straight sections as possible, before the curving area of the pocket.

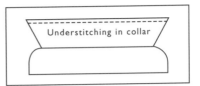

Topstitching

Topstitching is a technique to keep edges and seams flat and to help pleats hang smoothly. Stitching is worked from the right side of the garment through all thicknesses of fabric. The best method is to topstitch each section during the construction of the garment. A contrasting thread makes a decorative feature.

Knife-pleated skirt

1. Pin pleats in place on right side of garment (Fig A).
2. Tack pleats from top down and ½ inch (13 mm) in from pleat edge (Fig B).
3. Pin each pleat at the point where the topstitching will begin.
4. Stitch from bottom up towards the top, with the edge of the machine foot running level with the edge of the garment (Fig C).
5. Pull thread through to wrong side and tie (Fig D).

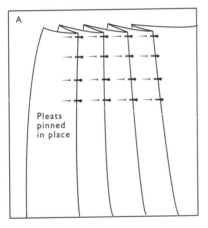

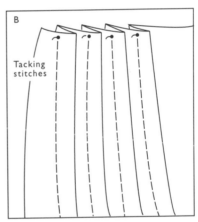

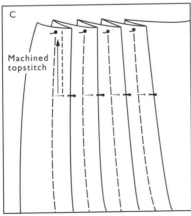

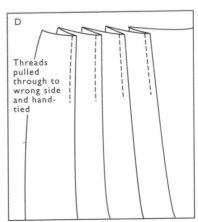

Peter Pan collar

1. Complete collar from instructions.
2. On the right side of the collar, outline with a marking pencil the exact width for topstitching.

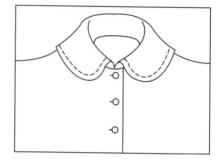

3. Change machine needle to a heavy duty size (the point of the needle is finer and will penetrate all the layers more easily).
4. Increase stitch length. Check the Needle and Thread Chart on page 13 for the correct thread to prevent the garment puckering.
5. When machining in the deep collar (strongly curved) area, it is helpful to pivot around the curves. Keep the machine needle down in the fabric, lift the pressure foot and turn slightly, lower foot and continue stitching to end of collar. This can be repeated several times.

Pointed collar

1. Follow the instructions for the Pater Pan collar.
2. You will only need to pivot once, at each corner.

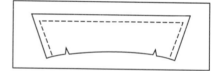

Jackets

1. The pattern for a topstitched jacket will stipulate the step-by-step stages of construction.
2. Before sewing, check the Needle and Thread Chart on page 13 for the correct thread to use on your fabric. Change to a heavy duty needle and select a stitch length a little longer than usual to accommodate the extra thicknesses.

3. Before topstitching remove any bulk from seams and interfacings to keep the right side of the garment even and flat.

Darts

Darts help mould a flat piece of material to the convex human shape. They also control and direct fullness. Darts are used at the bustline, back bodice, waist and hip areas.

Bodice darts

1. Before removing the pattern from the fabric, pin through the circle markings representing the darts on the wrong side of the fabric.
2. Lift the pattern up and mark the pin positions with tailor's chalk.
3. Fold the dart in half with the right sides of the fabric together, matching the chalk markings. Tailor tacks can also be used as a guide (Fig B).

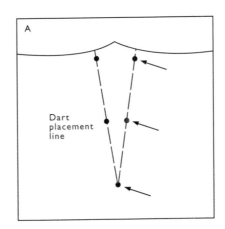

4. Press lightly along the foldline before stitching. This will help the dart to lie flat. Tack in place.
5. Always sew from the top of the dart down to the tip, never in the opposite direction. Do not reverse stitch at the end, but hand-knot the bottom threads to prevent puckering (Fig C).
6. Press darts flat on an ironing board. Refer back to the pattern guidesheet to see in which direction each dart is to lie after pressing (Fig D.)

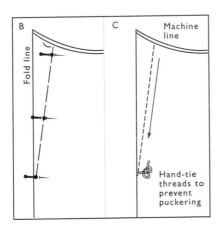

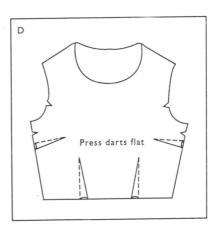

French darts

French darts are curved. They help to shape the waistline area where a garment has no waistline seam. French darts are only used in the front of a garment, never at the back.

1. Chalk the circle markings from the pattern onto the fabric and pin and tack in place on the wrong side.

2. Machine dart from end to point, and hand-knot thread ends. Do not machine-reverse at the end. Remove tacking.

3. Cut through the centre of the dart, from the wide end almost to the point. Be careful not to cut too close to the point or fraying will occur.

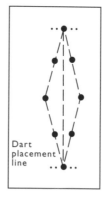
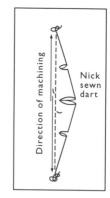

4. Clip seam allowance to let curve lie flat. Press flat.

Contour darts

A contour dart is a long single dart, double-ended. Its widest point fits at the waistline, then the dart tapers in both directions.

1. Chalk the circle markings from the pattern in place on the wrong side of the fabric.

2. Fold dart in half, matching chalk markings. Pin and tack in place.

3. Machine from the middle of the dart to one end. Go back to the middle and stitch to the other point. Tie thread ends and remove tacking.

4. Clip dart at waistline and each side. Press flat.

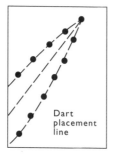
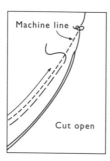
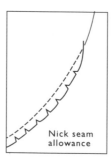
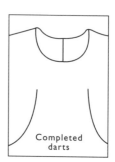

Bias strips

A bias cut is made when the fabric is cut on the diagonal, at 45° to the lengthwise and crosswise threads. Fabric cut on the true bias has maximum 'give', which helps shape garments. Avoid stretching the fabric when working with bias-cut pieces, and follow carefully all pattern markings.

Although commercial bias binding is readily available, bias binding made from the same fabric as the garment looks more professional, as everything matches. Remember, the inside of your garment should be as neat as the outside.

1. Fold a square or rectangle of fabric on the true diagonal, with the threads lining up exactly on the lengthwise and crosswise grains.

2. Cut along the fold to make the first cutting line. Before you go further remember, a strip of bias fabric 1 ½ inches (38 mm) wide is suitable for most items (Fig B).

3. To join bias strips, put right sides together, straight-grain raw edges together. Slide across until strips cross approximately ⅜ inch (1 cm) from corners. Stitch on straight grain from corner to corner (Fig C).

4. Trim seam to 3 inches (75 mm). Press open. Working from the right side of bias strip, press a narrow hem each side (Fig D).

5. Press the strip evenly in half down the middle. The bias binding is now ready to be used on a garment. (Fig E).

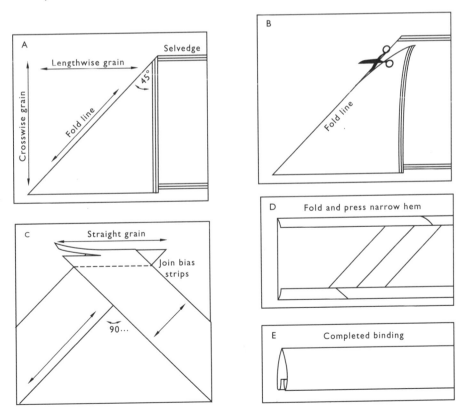

Bindings

Double Binding

Bindings are a neat and practical finish around necklines or sleeveless armholes. Made in a contrast colour they can give a very attractive finish. Make sure if you are using a colour contrast that the binding fabric is the same texture as the main fabric. This way the tension of the materials will be even and the bindings will lie flat. Check whether the fabric should be pre-washed to prevent shrinking later on.

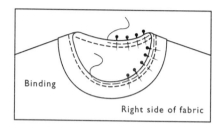

Binding

Right side of fabric

1. Measure the length of the area you are binding; allow 1 inch (25 mm) for seam allowance.

2. Cut bias strip 1 ¼ inches (31 mm) wide.

3. With the wrong sides together, press the binding in half.

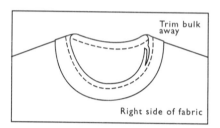

Trim bulk away

Right side of fabric

4. When binding a neckline, make the join at the shoulder; never make a join in the front or the back of the neckline. Armhole bindings should join at the sideseam under the arm.

5. Pin the binding on the right side of the garment, tack and machine along the seam line. Remove tacking.

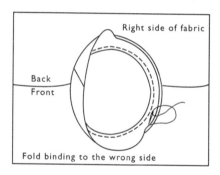

Right side of fabric

Back
Front

Fold binding to the wrong side

6. Trim seam allowance evenly and press the binding strip up towards the top.

7. Flip the binding over the raw edge to the wrong side of the garment. This forms what is called a 'wall' and must stand upright. Slipstitch a hem on the raw edge of the binding.

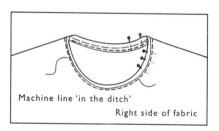

Machine line 'in the ditch'

Right side of fabric

8. On the right side of the garment, pin in the ditch, which means in the gutter of the seam directly

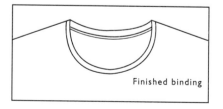

Finished binding

below the wall. Tack in place with matching thread; use bigger stitches at the back, as they are easier to remove.

9. Change the sewing machine foot to a zipper foot; this makes it easier to sew in the ditch and not on the binding. Remove tacking from back, cutting thread away.

10. Hold a shoulder pad under binding and press with a warm iron.

Rouleaus

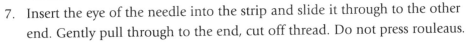

Rouleaus are ties or cylindrical strips of fabric. They are made from strips of material cut on the bias, which after machining are pulled through themselves to form ties. They are used for shoulder straps, and are traditionally used for the loops that fasten covered buttons on the backs of wedding and evening gowns in place of zipper openings. Hand-stitched into daisy flower shapes and beaded with tiny seed beads they give millinery, gowns and craft a fashionable finish.

1. To make shoulder straps, measure the length required for the strap plus a seam allowance.

2. Cut bias strips 1 inch (25 mm) wide and the length required.

3. Fold the strip in half, right sides together, so that the edges are even.

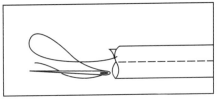

4. Stitch a ¼ inch (6 mm) seam along its length.

5. Thread a darning needle with fancywork cotton; for strength, make a small knot at the end.

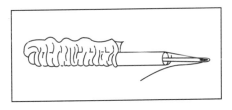

6. Sew thread through end of strip to fasten.

7. Insert the eye of the needle into the strip and slide it through to the other end. Gently pull through to the end, cut off thread. Do not press rouleaus.

Gathering

Gathering in a garment helps control fullness. It is used at waistlines and cuffs, sometimes in yokes and for making frills.

1. With the stitch length set at maximum, machine two lines of gathering stitches just above the seam line.

2. Insert a strong pin under a stitch and pull the thread up, then slide the fabric along the thread. Continue in this manner until all the gathers are even. It is easier to pull the gathering thread at intervals along the fabric than to pull the thread from end to end, as often it will snap.

3. To join the gathered section to another part of the garment, place the pins vertically, tack in place, then machine. Remove the tacking.

4. Press the gathers by working the point of the iron between the folds. Do not press across the gathers, as this flattens them.

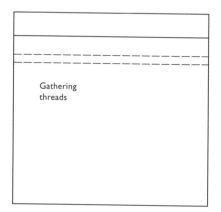

Gathering threads

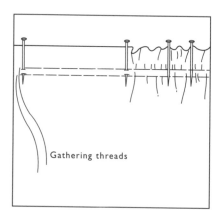

Gathering threads

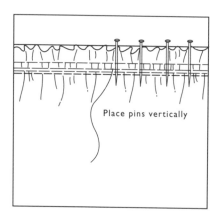

Place pins vertically

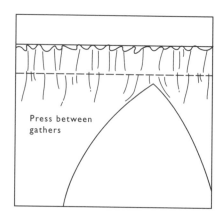

Press between gathers

Collars

Collars can add a particular fashion note to a garment. They are at eye contact level so finished detail must be exact. Pattern guides usually advise the correct interfacings to use with different fabrics. Interfacing is important, as it gives the added support needed for a professional finish. Corners and curves also can make or break a collar. Eliminate bulk in the seams by trimming the seam allowance from the interfacing before it is applied to the collar.

Pointed collar

1. Cut the iron-on interfacing pieces from the directions on the pattern guide sheet.
2. Trim away all seam allowances on interfacing to reduce bulk and press onto collar.
3. Join collar pieces with right sides facing together. Pin and tack in place on seam line and machine stitch.
4. Trim seam edges and cut corners on an angle to remove bulk.
5. Turn collar to right side and roll seam with your fingers. Press collar.
6. The collar is now ready to be fitted to your garment. Follow the pattern instructions carefully, and always tack in place.

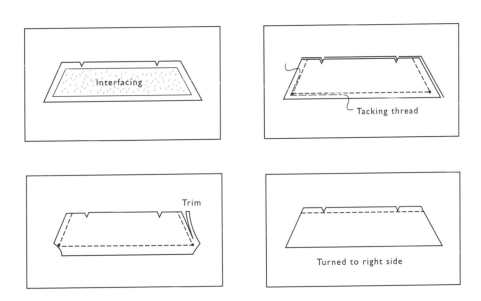

Peter Pan collar

The method outlined for the pointed collar applies to the Peter Pan collar, except that the rounded corners have to be nicked completely around the curves to make the collar hang perfectly flat. On the straight section of the collar sew a row of understitching. Press through each stage.

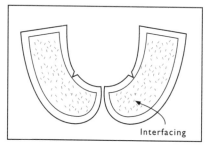

Interfacing

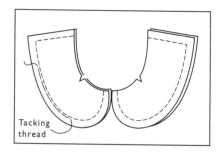

Tacking thread

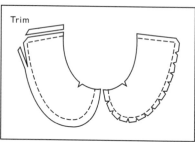

Trim

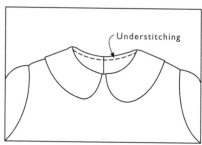

Understitching

Shirt collar

A shirt collar has a section called a collar stand. This section lies between the shirt and the collar and allows space for a tie to be worn. Some women's blouses also have a collar stand. They are a particularly smart finish to a blouse.

1. Follow the pointed collar instructions from step 1 to 5.
2. Apply interfacing to the wrong side of the collar stand piece.
3. With the right sides of the stand facing together, pin and tack between the two circle markings on the curved ends of the stand. Machine, trim curves and turn to the right side. Press flat.
4. With the right sides of the upper collar toward the rights side of the stand's facing, match and pin the collar to the stand. Tack through all the thicknesses along the seam line. Machine, remove tacking and turn to right side. Press flat.

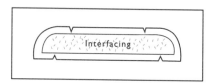

Interfacing

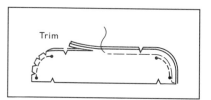

Trim

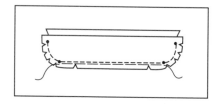

5. The collar is now ready to be stitched to the neckline. Follow instructions carefully.

Cuffs

Cuffs can give added flair to a garment. A basic black frock with contrasting white cuffs and collar can look extremely smart. Where the cuffs are joined with buttons, adding a buttonhole either side of the cuff and holding them together with cuff links can be an added fashion touch. Most cuffs open wider with a placket set into the sleeve.

Placket

1. Cut a bias fabric binding 1 ½ inches (40 mm) wide and twice the length of the marked placket on the sleeve, following the instructions on page 27.

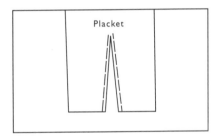

Placket

2. Machine a V-shaped row of stitching on the seam line where the opening has to be cut in the sleeve. Cut to the end of the opening.

3. With right sides of sleeve and bindings facing together, pin and tack along placket opening, machine, remove tacking and press seam flat.

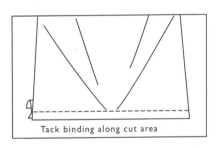

Tack binding along cut area

4. Fold binding to the wrong side, encasing raw edges. Fold the edge of the binding to meet the stitching line. Pin in place, tack, and machine close to the edge remove tacking.

5. Turn binding to wrong side of sleeve and press.

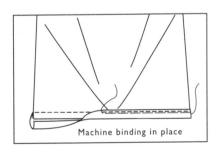

Machine binding in place

Cuff

1. Cut iron-on interfacing half the depth of the cuff, press in place on wrong side.

2. Fold cuff in half, right sides together.

3. At the right-hand end, machine down 1 ½ inches (4 cm), then across 1 ½ inches (4 cm). This is the section for the buttonhole. Trim the seam and cut seam corners on an angle to remove bulk.

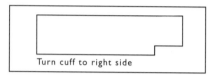

Turn cuff to right side

4. At the end of the cuff machine a ⅝ inch (1.5 cm) seam.

5. At the end of the overlap (buttonhole) section, cut up a little and turn cuff to the right side. Press flat.

6. Pin cuff to sleeve, matching nicks, rights sides together. Tack in place and machine. Remove tacking, trim seam edge.

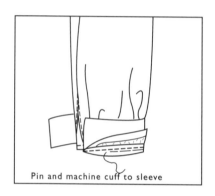

Pin and machine cuff to sleeve

7. Press seam allowance towards cuff. Bring folded edge of sleeve facing to stitching line on wrong side of sleeve.

8. Pin and tack. Machine topstitch in place close to the edge.

9. Remove tacking and press cuff, holding a shoulder pad underneath to prevent creasing.

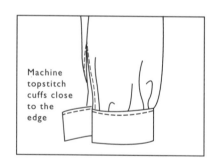

Machine topstitch cuffs close to the edge

Waistband

Check that the waistband pattern is the right length for your waist measurement. Allow a little extra in the length, if need be, for tucking in a blouse and for comfort.

1. A waistband is best cut on the length of the material. This gives the least amount of stretch and is stronger.
2. Cut a strip of iron-on interfacing half the width of the waistband pattern. Cut off seam allowance to prevent bulkiness.
3. Press the interfacing onto the wrong side of the material (Fig A).

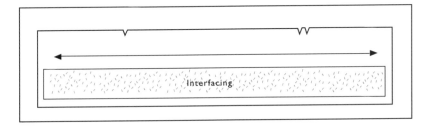

4. Fold the band in half with right sides together.
5. At the right-hand edge, stitch down 1 ½ inches(4 cm), then 1 ½ inches(4 cm) across to make the buttonhole section. Cut away excess fabric under this area. Trim the seam and cut seam corners on an angle to remove the bulk (Fig B).

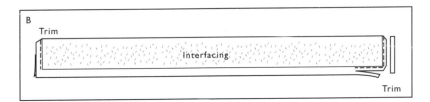

6. At the left-hand end sew a ⅝ inch (1.5 cm) seam.
7. Turn the waistband to the right side and press flat.
8. When joining the waistband to the skirt, turn skirt inside out and pin the right side of the waistband to the wrong side of the skirt.
9. Tack in place and machine. Trim away any bulk. Press the seam up towards the waistband.
10. Flip the waistband up and over the seam allowance to the right side of the garment.
11. Press the seam allowance and pin all along the edge of the waistband with the pins placed vertically (this prevents puckering).
12. Tack in place a little above the edge (Fig C).

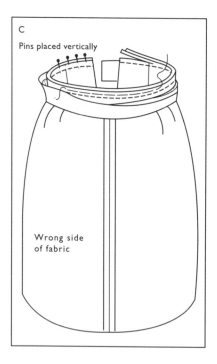

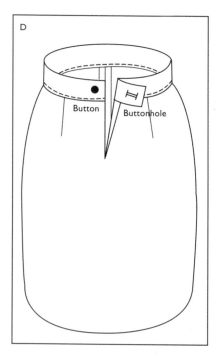

13. Machine close to the edge. Remove the tacking.

14. Press the waistband flat

15. Make a buttonhole in the overlap area or attach fasteners (Fig D).

Setting in a zip

The lapped application method is used in skirts and frocks. Side zips are sewn in on the left, so the lap section is facing towards the back and you cannot look directly at the teeth. Use the zipper foot attachment on your machine to help you sew close to the zipper edge. Test the zip before you use it by pulling it up and down to make sure it runs freely. Remember, you must always tack a zip in place and the teeth should never be visible when wearing your garment.

THREE POINTS TO REMEMBER:

- tack a zip in place
- use a zipper foot
- pull the head of the zip down out of the way until you pass that sewing area.

1. Follow your pattern's instructions on how your zip seam area should be completed before setting in your zip (Fig A).

2. Pull your zip up and down to test it is not faulty.

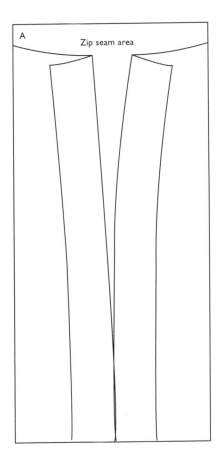

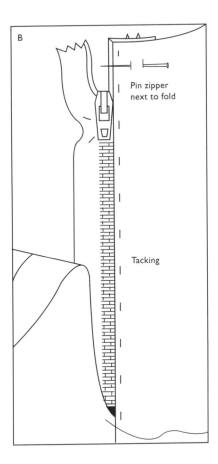

3. With the right side of the garment facing you, fold over each side of the top of the zip, hand stitch in place.

4. Still with the right side of the garment facing you, pin the closed zip from top to bottom next to the fold on the right hand side. On the other side (which now becomes the lap side) pin the zip ¼ inch (6 mm) from the fold line from bottom to top.

5. Tack the zip in place to prevent it from moving, sewing bigger tacking stitches at the back (they are easier to remove). Use the same colour thread as your garment. The little tacking stitches, which are now visible on the right side, will help as a guide to sew straight (Fig B).

6. Put zipper foot in position on your machine. Check that there is enough thread in the bobbin to complete the sewing of the section of the zip in one step.

7. Start machining from the top of the lap side. First, pull the zip down ¾ inch (2 cm) and sew this section. Lift the pressure foot, pull the zipper head back up and lower the foot, and then continue sewing down to the bottom of the zip. (Fig C)

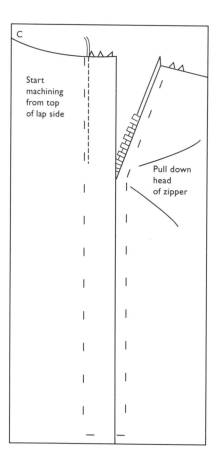

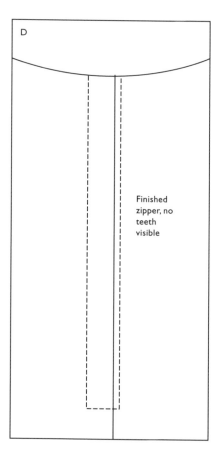

8. Pivot the fabric to sew across the bottom of the zip. Pivot again before going up the other side.

9. Continue sewing up towards the top. Stop ¾ inch (2 cm) away from the top and pull the zipper head down and out of the way before sewing up to the top.

10. Remove tacking from the back, cutting threads out (Fig D).

11. Stitch a hook at the top of the zip on the flap side, a little back from the edge. Sewing with a double thread and a knot, again a little back from the edge, make a double loop the size of the hook and blanket-stitch along its length. The hook and eye should not be visible when the person is wearing the garment.

12. Place a cloth over the zip and press lightly.

Sleeves

Set-in sleeve

A set-in sleeve is a very tailored sleeve moulded into the armhole with no gathers. The sleeve pattern will have one notch at the front of the sleeve and two notches at the back. The back of the sleeve has extra measurement to allow for the movement of the body.

1. Using the largest stitch on your machine, sew a gathering row on the seam line at the top of the sleeve, starting at the front notch and going around to the two back notches.
2. Stitch the underarm seam, neaten and press flat open.
3. Turn the sleeve to the right side.
4. Hold the garment so you are looking into the armhole. Drop the sleeve into the armhole, right sides facing each other.
5. Match the seam lines and notches together. Pin top of sleeve to the shoulder seam, underarm seam to underarm seam, notches to notches. The area between the notches is where you ease in the sleeve.

   Because the sleeve is slightly larger than the armhole at this stage, use the gathering thread to slightly ease the material to fit neatly into the armhole. The gathering thread is only to mould the sleeve head in place. There should be no puckering.
6. Tack in place all around the armhole.
7. Machine a little below the tacking, then remove the tacking, being careful not to stretch the armhole.

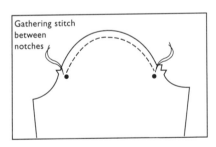

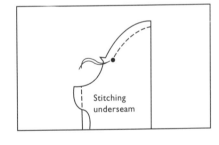

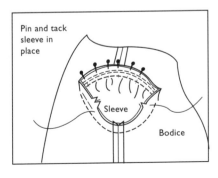

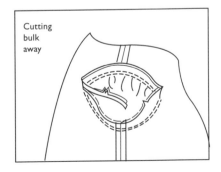

8. Sew a second row of stitching ¼ inch (6 mm) away from the sewing line, within the seam allowance.

9. Trim any bulk away.

10. Press armhole seam (holding shoulder pad underneath) down towards the bottom of sleeve.

Shirt sleeve

Shirt sleeves have no gather as they have a much lower sleeve cap curve. A shirt sleeve is sewn to the body of the garment before the side seams are sewn together. The same method is used for a garment with dropped shoulders.

1. On the top of the sleeve seam allowance, run a gathering stitch by machine between the front armhole notch and the two back notches.

2. With right sides together, pin the sleeve to the armhole edge of the bodice, matching all notches.

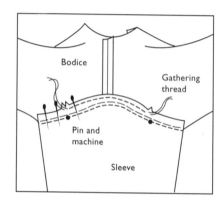

3. Use the gathering thread to ease the sleeve in the area between the nicks, the same way as the set-in sleeve. Make sure you have no folds; the easing is only to mould the sleeve into place in the armhole.

4. Tack, then machine stitch in place all around the armhole section. Remove tacking.

5. Neaten the seam, cut any bulk away. Machine another row of stitching in the same allowance, ¼ inch (6 mm) from the sleeve stitching.

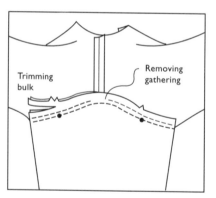

6. Press seam down towards bottom of garment.

7. Pin, tack and machine the side seams of the garment; neaten edges. Press seam towards the back.

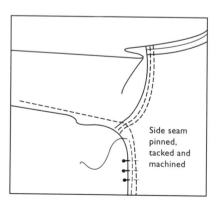

Raglan sleeve

The raglan sleeve is sewn to the garment in one continuous seam, which runs from the neckline to the underarm. If a shoulder dart is marked on the pattern it will help the sleeve to fit and hang correctly.

1. Mark dart position (if any) with tailor's chalk. Pin and tack in place. Machine from top to bottom of dart. Tie thread ends and remove tacking.

2. Press dart flat, then cut through centre nearly to the end of the dart to help it lie flat.

3. From the top of the sleeves, pin the diagonal seams of the sleeves to the bodice with right sides together, matching the notches.

4. Tack in place and machine. Remove tacking.

5. Trim seam and cut small nicks evenly spaced about 1 inch (25 mm) along edge of seam. Press seam open.

6. Pin the side seams of the garment, from the end of the sleeve down to the waistline. Machine.

7. Cut nicks 1 inch (25 mm) apart in curved area of the underarm. Neaten edges and press seam flat towards the back.

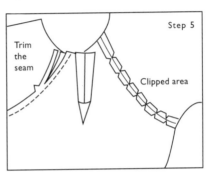
Step 5
Trim the seam
Clipped area

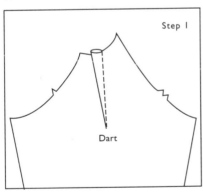
Step 1
Dart

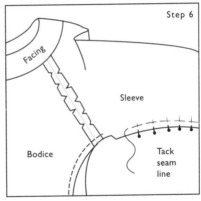
Step 6
Facing
Sleeve
Bodice
Tack seam line

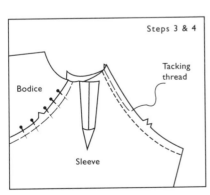
Steps 3 & 4
Bodice
Tacking thread
Sleeve

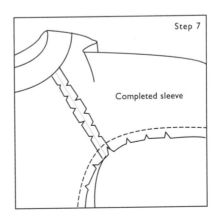
Step 7
Completed sleeve

Pockets

Pockets are not only functional, but in different shapes and sizes can be another feature trim. They are sewn on the garment while it is flat open, before side seams are sewn together.

1. Always follow the pattern guide instructions carefully.
2. Make sure pairs of pockets are the same shape and size.
3. The pattern will indicate a placement line to be marked on the garment.
4. Always pin and baste pockets onto the garment to keep them absolutely straight.
5. Trim away any bulk and press well at each step.

Patch pockets

1. Use tailor's chalk to mark the pocket placement line on the garment.
2. Press top edge of pocket under ¼ inch (6 mm).
3. Turn top of pocket to outside on hemline. Starting at hem fold, stitch around raw edges at ⅝ inch (15 mm).
4. Cut corners diagonally to remove bulk.
5. Turn hem to inside. Press under seam allowance below hem on line of stitching.
6. Machine hem in place.

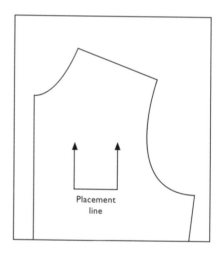

Placement line

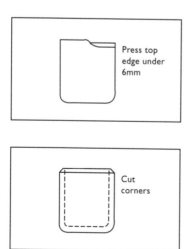

Press top edge under 6mm

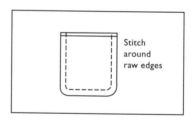

Stitch around raw edges

Cut corners

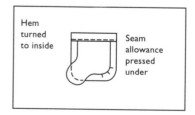

Hem turned to inside

Seam allowance pressed under

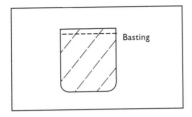

Basting

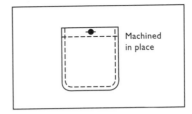

Machined in place

7. Pin pocket on placement line and baste to keep pocket on grainline.

8. Machine in place close to the edge and press flat.

9. If the pocket has a button and buttonhole, the buttonhole is sewn before stitching the pocket to the garment. The button is sewn in place last.

Pleats

Pleats control fullness and give a lot of body comfort to the wearer. The style of pleating you choose will depend on the pattern requirements, the choice of fabric and your figure.

Knife pleats

Knife pleats hang in a very soft line. They all run in the same direction. They can be pressed from the waistline down to the second hip measurement, or be pressed all the way to the hemline.

Box pleats

Box pleats are a traditional style of pleating. They were nearly always used in school uniforms until quite recently. The two folds of each pleat are turned away from each other.

Inverted pleats

Inverted pleats are two folds that meet evenly at the centre of the waist and face each other. The line of a skirt with inverted pleats can be very slimming, as the hip area has no pleats.

Hand-sewing

Any hand-sewing for the finished stages of a garment must be very neat. Use fine sewing needles and the correct matching cotton. The less hand-sewing there is the more professional the finished garment will look.

Hemstitching

Hemstitching is an invisible stitch suitable for hems and sleeve edges, particularly on sheer and silk fabrics to help the garment hang properly and have a professional finish.

1. Level the hemline carefully and press raw edge up ½ inch (13 mm) to the wrong side. Machine stitch close to this edge.
2. Turn up the hem allowance placing pins vertically all around the hemline.
3. Thread a fine sewing needle with matching cotton, make a tiny knot at the end.
4. Start from right to left at the seam line and fasten the knot in place under the fold. Picking up hardly any threads of the garment, pull thread through and run the needle along the top of folded edge to form a stitch. Continue all the way around the hem.
5. Finish with a backstitch in the fold area. Press hem flat on wrong side with a press cloth.

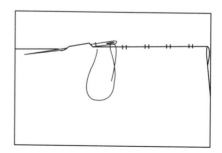

Slipstitching

Slipstitching is an almost invisible stitch, which when properly done cannot be seen on the right side of the garment. When hemming a sheer or silk fabric, a slipped hem is advisable, as it will help the fabric hang properly.

1. Level the hemline carefully. Press the raw edge up ½ inch (13 mm) to the wrong side. Machine stitch close to the edge.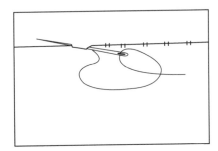

2. Turn up the hem allowance, placing the pins vertically all around the hemline.

3. Thread a fine sewing needle with matching cotton and make a tiny knot at the end.

4. Starting from right to left at the seam line, fasten the knot in place under the fold. Picking up hardly any threads of the fabric, pull the thread through and then through a few threads of the fold edge. Continue in this way all around the hem.

5. Finish the hem with a backstitch in the fold area.

6. Press the hem flat on the wrong side.

Buttonholes

Machine buttonholes

Buttonholes can easily be made with a sewing machine if you have a buttonhole foot. Follow the guide in your sewing machine manual. Practise on as many types and thicknesses of fabric as you can. Remember to adjust the tension on your machine when you are sewing thick fabrics. Keep practising until your buttonholes look professional. The rule is that buttonholes are sewn on right side over left for women's clothes and left side over right for men's clothes.

Hand-sewn buttonholes

1. Measure the width of the button before you mark the size of the buttonhole. Buttons are not completely flat, so you must allow for the 'rise'.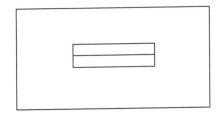

2. On the right side of the garment mark the position of the

buttonhole and its length.

3. Using only the point of your scissors, cut through all thicknesses of fabric between the end markings. Insert the point of the scissors at the centre and cut to one end, then cut to the other end.

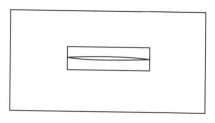

4. Using thread to match the fabric, thread a needle with double thread, with a small knot at the end. Allow enough length for the complete buttonhole.

5. Secure the thread underneath the slit at the top. Bring the thread to the front from right to left under the point of the needle and draw through the loop so the little knot is at the edge of the slit. Continue this buttonhole stitch along one cut edge, and then along the other.

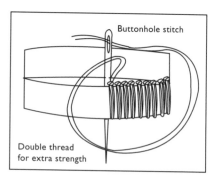

Buttonhole stitch

Double thread for extra strength

6. At each end of the buttonhole sew a bar of horizontal stitches to reinforce and complete the buttonhole.

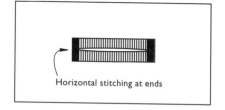

Horizontal stitching at ends

Sewing on buttons

As well as being functional, buttons can give a very smart finish to a garment. On a very tailored garment, for example, buttons properly selected can give a finish as smart as adding jewellery or accessories.

Sew-through buttons

1. Pattern guides often contain a specially marked strip, which can be pinned to your garment to give you the correct placement for the button. Remember, buttons go left

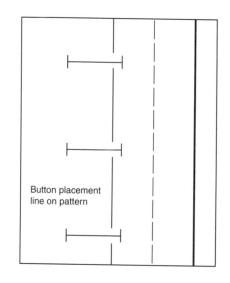

Button placement line on pattern

under right for women's clothes, right under left for men's (this matches the buttonholes).

2. Place a pin right through the centre of the buttonhole. Using a double thread and a knot, make a backstitch on the pin mark.

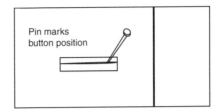

3. Stitch the button in place, sewing in and out through the holes at least four times.

4. Reinforce the strength of the stitching by winding the thread around the stitches, underneath the button. This makes a 'shank' and raises the button a little from the fabric. Backstitch to secure the thread and cut close to the garment.

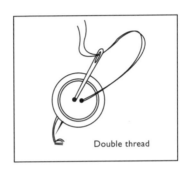

Shank buttons

Shank buttons have a ring at the back of the button. They are essential on garments like woollen overcoats, men's waistcoats and blazers. Covered buttons have a back ring as well — they are often designed to be used on the backs of wedding gowns, instead of a zip. They can also be used on the wrist opening of long classical sleeves.

1. Mark the position for the button on the right side of the garment.

2. Remember, as for sew-through buttons, it is left under right for women's clothes and right under left for men's.

3. With a strong double thread and a knot, make a backstitch where the button is to be sewn. Space the thread a little way from the ring.

4. Stitch in and out the ring at least four times to secure. Wind the thread from the ring down to the garment. (This extra 'length' for the shank is essential when working with heavy woollen fabrics and other thick fabrics.) Backstitch to secure thread and cut close to the garment.

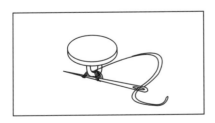

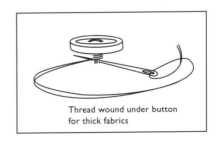

Thread wound under button
for thick fabrics

Hooks and eyes

Hooks and eyes are used where two edges need to be held together. They come in a variety of sizes. A larger size is best used on waistlines where there is extra strain on the garment. Loop eyes and straight eyes are available.

Edges which meet

A neater finish for a neckline closing is obtained by making your own 'eye' from thread, 'buttonholing' along a doubled length of thread in the required position. The hook and eye should never be visible when joined.

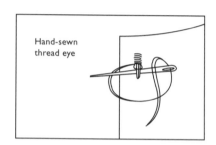

Hand-sewn thread eye

Overlapping edges

1. On a waistband, for example, place the hook on the inside of the overlap about ¼ inch (6 mm) in from the edge.
2. Stitch around each 'hole' with a buttonhole stitch.
3. Pass the needle through the middle of the hook, then stitch over it three or four times to hold it flat against the fabric.
4. Mark the position of the eye on the other side of the garment, placing a pin where the end of the hook falls.
5. Stitch a straight eye in place with a buttonhole stitch around each hole.

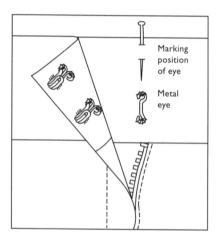

Marking position of eye

Metal eye

1/2 inch (1.3 cm) seam allowance

1/2 inch (1.3 cm)

Seam line

Seam line

Back
Cut 1 on fo

old

PATTERNS

Centre fold

Centre fold

Yoke
Cut 2

Seam line

Hem line

m line

back
Centre

3/4 inch

Grain line

Cutting line

Cutting line

Centre
nt

Fold

seam allowance

1/2 inch (1.3 cm)

Seam line

Fold

Grain

Grain

Patterns
Pinafore

*A pinafore is always a very comfortable garment to wear.
This black and red pinafore is a very easy pattern to follow
and takes very little time to sew.*

Materials:

2 ¼ yards (2.1 m) black and white cotton fabric, 45 inches (115 cm) wide
1 yard (1 m) red cotton for bindings, 45 inches (115 cm) wide
1 reel of black cotton polyester thread
1 reel of red cotton polyester thread.

Method:

1. Pin and tack shoulder seams of front and back bodices together, machine and remove tacking. Press seams together towards the back. Overlock the seams.

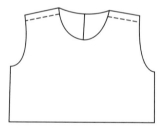

1. Machine front to back at shoulders.

2. Tack and machine the red bias bindings around the neckline and the armholes. (Refer to bindings on page 28.)

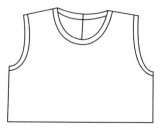

2. Machine red bias binding around neckline and armholes.

3. With right sides of bodice facing together, join the side seams and overlock the edges. Press the seams towards the back.

4. With right sides of the skirt facing together, pin and tack and machine side seams. Overlock edges and press towards the back.

5. Press up a ¾ inch (2 cm) hem at the bottom of the skirt.

6. Measure the width of the hem of the skirt and cut a 4 ½ inch (115 mm) strip from the red material plus ¾ inch (2 cm) for a seam. Join strip to right side and press in half. Overlock the edge of the strip. Pin strip to the skirt under the pressed ¾ inch (2 cm) hem matching join of the strip at the side seam of the skirt. Tack and machine.

7. Sew a gathering stitch ¾ inch (2 cm) from the top edge pull up gathering stitch to fit the bodice.

8. With right sides of the bodice and skirt together, pin centre of bodice to centre of skirt, match side seams then evenly distribute gathers all the way around. Place pins vertically in between the folds.

9. Tack and machine and overlock the edges. Press up towards the bodice.

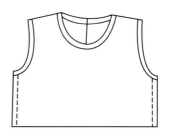

3. Machine side seams.

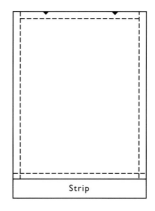

4. Machine side seams of skirt — join strip to hem.

Machine a gathering at waist of skirt. Join bodice to skirt. Machine zipper in back seam.

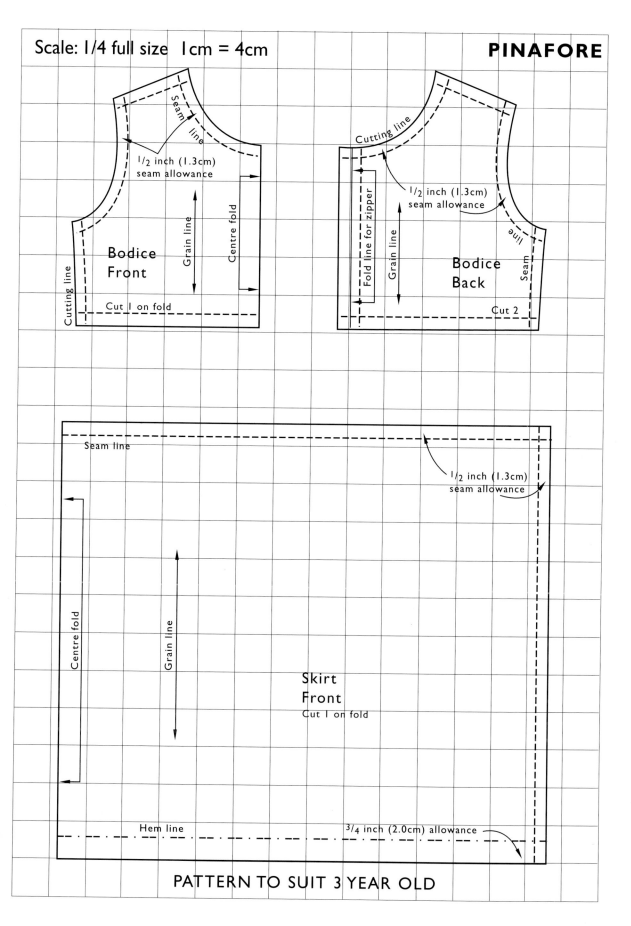

Scale: 1/4 full size 1cm = 4cm

PINAFORE

Seam line

1/2 inch (1.3cm) seam allowance

Grain line

Centre fold

Bodice Front

Cutting line

Cut 1 on fold

Cutting line

Fold line for zipper

1/2 inch (1.3cm) seam allowance

Grain line

Bodice Back

Seam line

Cut 2

Seam line

1/2 inch (1.3cm) seam allowance

Centre fold

Grain line

Skirt Front

Cut 1 on fold

Hem line

3/4 inch (2.0cm) allowance

PATTERN TO SUIT 3 YEAR OLD

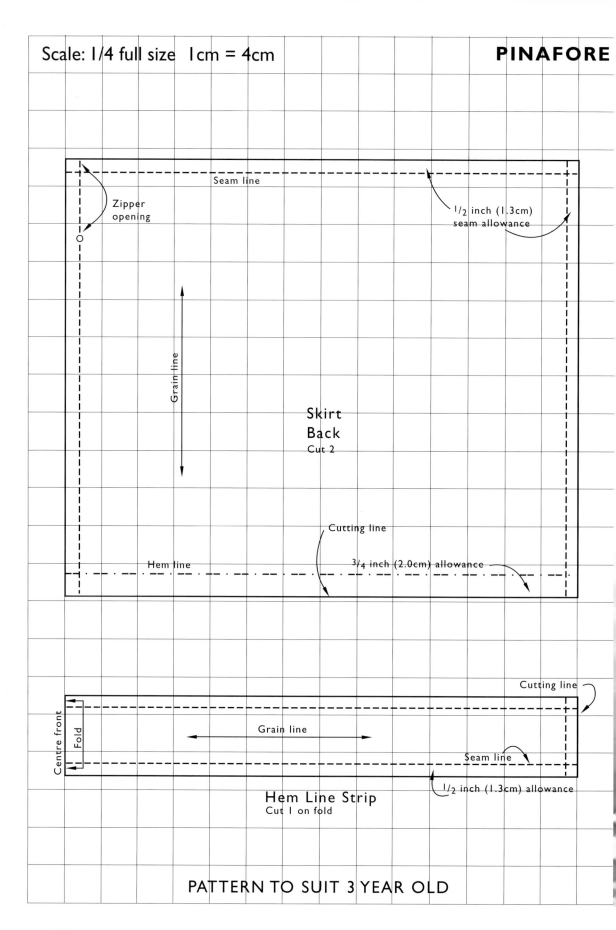

Scale: 1/4 full size 1cm = 4cm

PINAFORE

Seam line

Zipper opening

1/2 inch (1.3cm) seam allowance

Grain line

Skirt
Back
Cut 2

Cutting line

Hem line

3/4 inch (2.0cm) allowance

Centre front

Fold

Grain line

Cutting line

Seam line

1/2 inch (1.3cm) allowance

Hem Line Strip
Cut 1 on fold

PATTERN TO SUIT 3 YEAR OLD

Lace Blouse

You will always feel special when you wear this beaded lace blouse over a satin camisole and matching skirt. This blouse has scalloped edges on the hemline and the sleeves, this is optional depending on your lace.

Materials:

2 ½ yards (2.3 m) lace 45 inches (115 cm) wide
1 reel matching polyester thread
6 medium size cream buttons
packet silver crystal beads
matching beading thread.

Method:

1. Machine a gathering stitch on the seam line of one yoke (the remaining yoke section is the facing).

2. Turn in seam allowance on front edges of yoke back facing and press.

3. Pin right side of yoke back facing to wrong side of the back, machine. Press the seam towards the yoke.

1. Machine a gathering stitch on the seam line of the yoke.

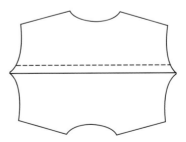

2. Machine right side of yoke back and front yoke together.

4. Pin front edges of yoke to upper edges of the front. Machine, keeping pressed edges of yoke facing over seams. Tack raw edges together.

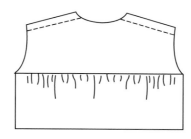

3. Machine front edges of yoke to upper edges of the front.

5. With the two front sections facing together, machine seam from dot down to the bottom. Press the seam flat open. Overlock the edges.
6. Measure the size needed for the loops around one pearl button. Cut and stitch loops evenly in the opening front, on the right hand side. Pin and tack facing to the right side. Machine. Press flat. Press left side seam flat.

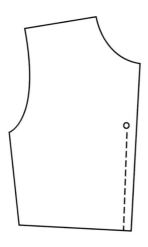

4. Machine the two front sections facing together. Machine seam from circle down to the hemline.

5. Stitch loops evenly on the right hand side of the front opening.

BEADING THE COLLAR

7. Thread the bead needle with double thread and stitch a crystal bead in the centre of each lace flower on the collar, but not into the seam line.

6. Stitch a crystal bead in the centre of each lace flower on top section of the blouse. Tack and machine lace scalloped edge to the collar — right sides facing.

8. With right side of collar facing, pin, tack and machine on the seam line of the collar the scalloped edging. With right side of collar and back collar facing machine together. Turn to right side. (Press only on the edge to avoid the beading.)

9. Pin and tack collar to the neck edge and machine. Cut a lace bias binding strip (see page 27 for instructions).

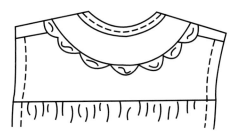

7. Machine the two collar sections together — turn to right side. Machine collar to neck edge, and machine a lace binding across the seam. Machine down side seams.

10. Machine down side seams. Overlock edges and press.

11. Set in the sleeves (see page 39 for setting in a sleeve)

12. Machine seam of the scalloped edge. With right sides of hem and scalloped edging, pin, tack and machine. Overlock the edge.

13. Stitch each pearl button in the centre of each loop.

8. Set in the sleeves. Machine scalloped edge to the hemline. Stitch a pearl button in the centre of each loop.

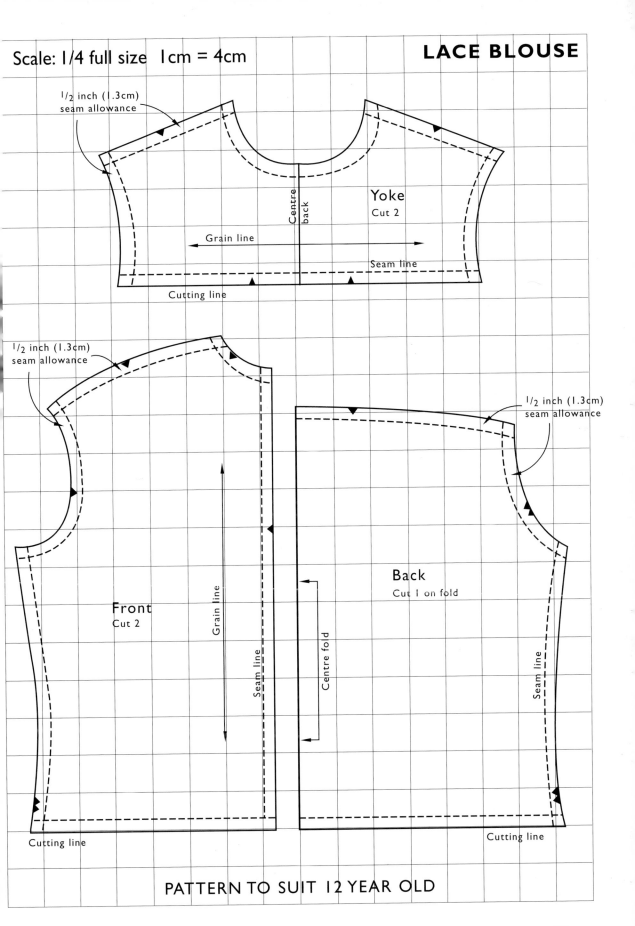

Scale: 1/4 full size   1cm = 4cm

LACE BLOUSE

1/2 inch (1.3cm) seam allowance

Yoke
Cut 2

Centre back

Grain line

Seam line

Cutting line

1/2 inch (1.3cm) seam allowance

1/2 inch (1.3cm) seam allowance

Front
Cut 2

Grain line

Seam line

Back
Cut 1 on fold

Centre fold

Seam line

Cutting line

Cutting line

PATTERN TO SUIT 12 YEAR OLD

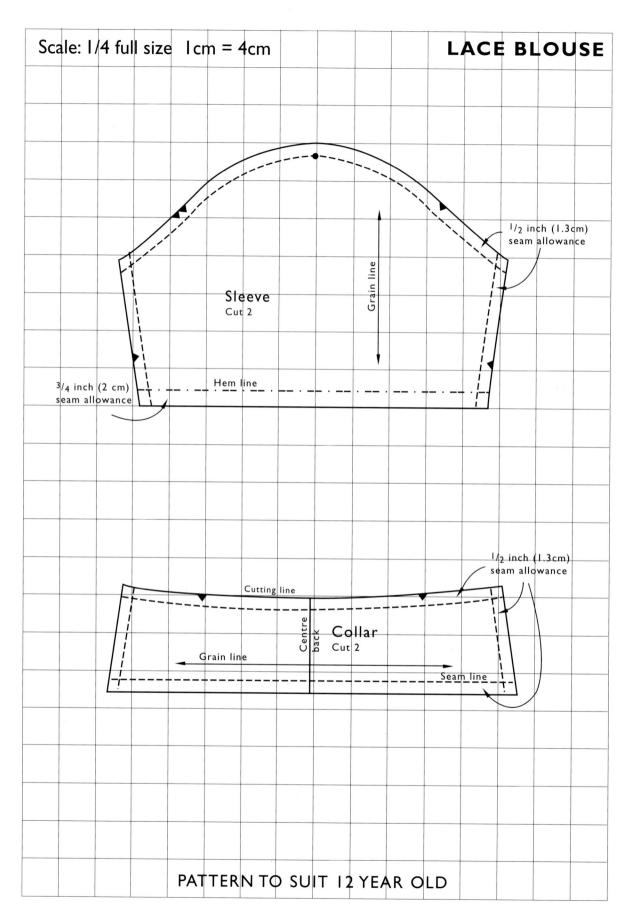

Scale: 1/4 full size 1cm = 4cm

LACE BLOUSE

1/2 inch (1.3cm)
seam allowance

Grain line

Sleeve
Cut 2

3/4 inch (2 cm)
seam allowance

Hem line

1/2 inch (1.3cm)
seam allowance

Cutting line

Centre back

Collar
Cut 2

Grain line

Seam line

PATTERN TO SUIT 12 YEAR OLD

Camisole

Materials:

1 ½ yards (1.2 m) satin material, 45 inches (115 cm) wide

1 reel matching polyester thread

Method:

1. Machine a bias binding strip to the front and back necklines 1 ¾ yards (1.6 m) strip for both. (Refer to Bias binding strips on page 27.)

2. Machine front and back together at the side seams. Overlock the edges and press seams towards the back.

3. Repeat bias binding instructions for the shoulder straps, measure the length needed.

4. On the inside, pin shoulder straps to the upper edges of the front and back on the circle markings.

5. Try the camisole on and adjust the straps to fit. Tuck in raw ends of the strap and slip stitch.

6. Neatly slip stitch straps to the camisole.

7. Press up a ¾ inch (2 cm) hem at the edge of the camisole and machine close to the edge.

1. Machine a bias binding strip to front and back necklines. Machine front and back together at side seams.

2. Repeat bias binding instructions for the shoulder straps.
3. Slip stitch straps to camisole. Press up hem and machine close to the edge.

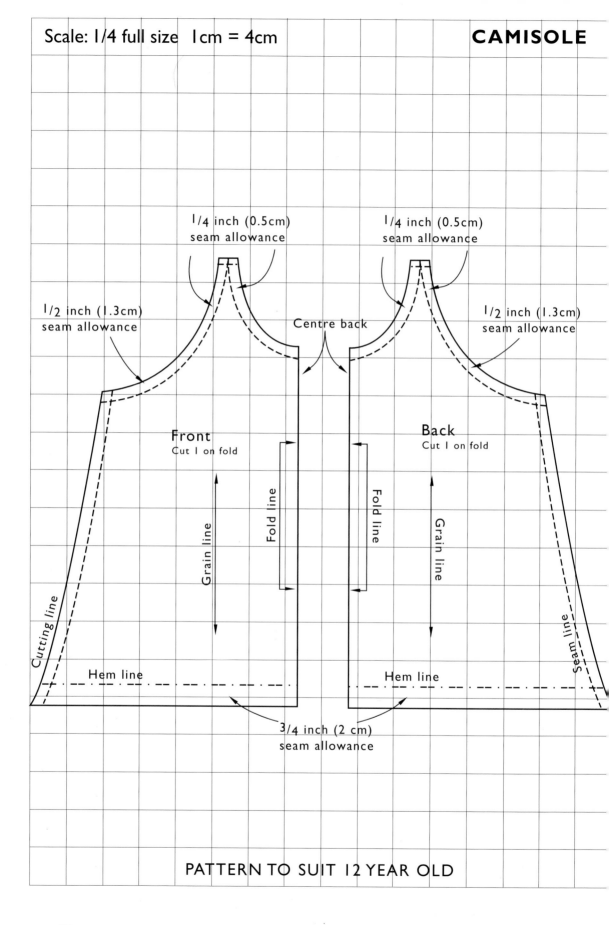

Scale: 1/4 full size 1cm = 4cm

CAMISOLE

1/4 inch (0.5cm) seam allowance

1/4 inch (0.5cm) seam allowance

1/2 inch (1.3cm) seam allowance

Centre back

1/2 inch (1.3cm) seam allowance

Front
Cut 1 on fold

Back
Cut 1 on fold

Grain line

Fold line

Fold line

Grain line

Cutting line

Seam line

Hem line

Hem line

3/4 inch (2 cm)
seam allowance

PATTERN TO SUIT 12 YEAR OLD

Frilled Skirt

Materials:

2 ½ yards (2.3 m) silk material, 45 inches (115 cm) wide

7 inch (18 cm) matching zip

1 reel matching silk thread

Method:

1. Pin and tack the darts in the skirt, machine each dart from the upper edge towards the point. Tie off threads at the points. Press the darts towards the centre back.

2. With right sides of back and front facing together, pin and tack side seams leaving the left side open for zip above the circle. Press the seam flat open and overlock the edges.

3. Set in the zip. (Refer to Setting in a zip on page 36)

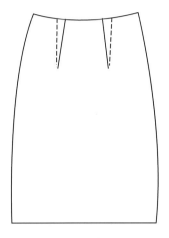

1. Tack and machine back darts. Press the darts towards the centre back.

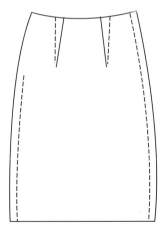

2. Tack and machine side seams. Leave zipper opening on the left side. Overlock seams and press the seams open.

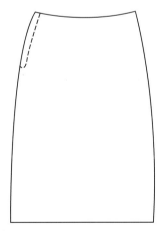

3. Tack and machine the zipper in the left.

4. Lay the front facing piece on the back facing piece so the right sides are together. Machine the right side seam to correspond to the skirt. Press the seam open, overlock the lower edge of the facing.

5. Tack the facing to the upper edge of the skirt, with the right sides facing and matching the side seams. Turn under side edges of the facing at the zip side. Machine upper edge of the facing to the skirt. Trim the seams and clip the curves.

6. Turn the facing to the inside. Tack the seam edge and press. Stitch the narrow edge to the zip by hand.

7. Pin the frill to the bottom of the skirt hemline to measure exactly where the one seam of the frill will be joined at the right side seam of the skirt.

8. Remove the pins and machine and overlock the seam of the frill and press. On the top of the frill and on the seam line machine with a large stitch a row of stitching (this helps the 'hang' of the frill when sewn to the hemline but it does not have gathers). Overlock the lower edge of the frill and press a ¼ inch (6 mm) hem and machine close to the edge.

9. With right side of the frill and skirt hemline pin and tack seam of the skirt. Machine all around the edge. Trim the seam, overlock and press.

4. Join the front facing seam, press seam open. Overlock edge, and overlock lower edge.

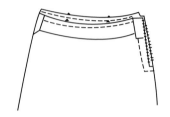

5. Tack and machine the facing to the upper edge of the skirt.

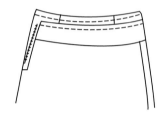

6. Turn facing to the inside, handstitch the narrow edges of the facing near the zipper.

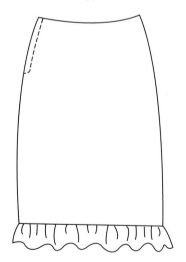

7. Tack and machine and overlock the seam of the frill. Overlock the bottom edge of the frill and press up ½ inch (13 mm). Hem and machine close to the edge. Pin, tack and machine frill to the skirt hem line, matching the join with the seam line.

Scale: 1/4 full size 1cm = 4cm

FRILLED SKIRT

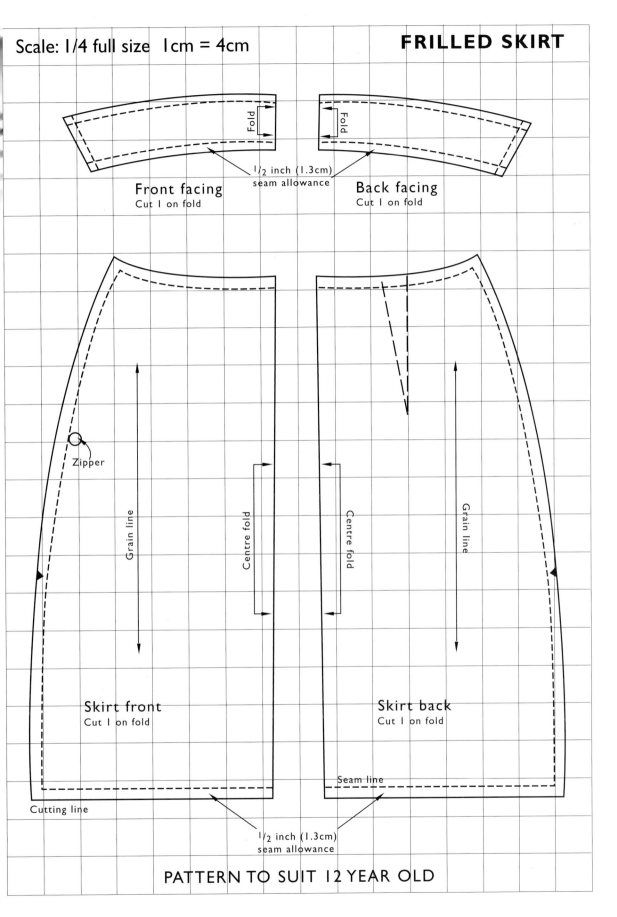

Front facing
Cut 1 on fold

Back facing
Cut 1 on fold

Fold

Fold

1/2 inch (1.3cm)
seam allowance

Zipper

Grain line

Centre fold

Centre fold

Grain line

Skirt front
Cut 1 on fold

Skirt back
Cut 1 on fold

Seam line

Cutting line

1/2 inch (1.3cm)
seam allowance

PATTERN TO SUIT 12 YEAR OLD

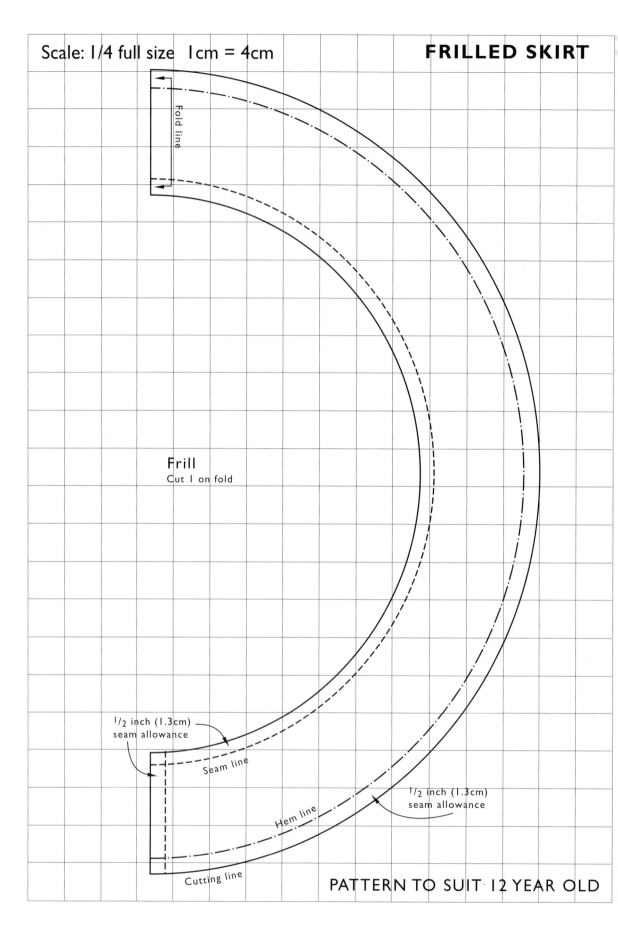

Scale: 1/4 full size   1cm = 4cm

FRILLED SKIRT

Fold line

Frill
Cut 1 on fold

1/2 inch (1.3cm)
seam allowance

Seam line

1/2 inch (1.3cm)
seam allowance

Hem line

Cutting line

PATTERN TO SUIT 12 YEAR OLD

Emerald Satin A-Line Gown

This is an elegant and fashionable frock for a special occasion. The shape is a simple A-line, lined with matching taffeta.

Materials:

1 ¾ yards (1.5 m) satin material, 45 inches (115 cm) wide
1 ¾ yards (1.5 m) taffeta, 45 inches (115 cm) wide
1 reel of matching polyester thread.

Method:

1. With right sides of front and back facing together, machine the side seams. Press seams towards the back and overlock the edges. Repeat with the lining.

2. Machine two rouleaus 10 inches (26 cm) long for each shoulder strap. (Refer to Rouleaus on page 29.)

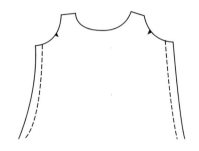

1. Machine side seams with right side of front and back facing. Press seams towards the back.

2. Machine rouleau straps.

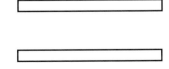

3. Turn rouleau straps to right side.

4. Tack each strap to upper edge of front.

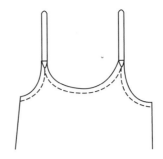

5. With right sides of frock and lining facing, machine neckline and armholes. Understitch edge of slip around neck and armholes.

3. Tack each shoulder strap to upper edge of the front.

4. With right side of the frock and right side of the lining slip, tack and machine all around the neckline and armholes. Trim away bulk from seams. Press seams towards the top and turn frock out to the right side.

5. Under stitch edge of the slip close to the seam through the seam allowance.

6. Pin ends of strap to the back. Try on and adjust to fit. Hand stitch securely in place.

7. Measure and level hem evenly, overlock the edge and press up a ¾ inch (2 cm) hem and machine close to the edge.

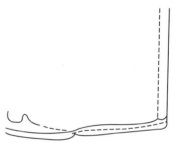

6. Handstitch straps to the back and machine hem close to the edge.

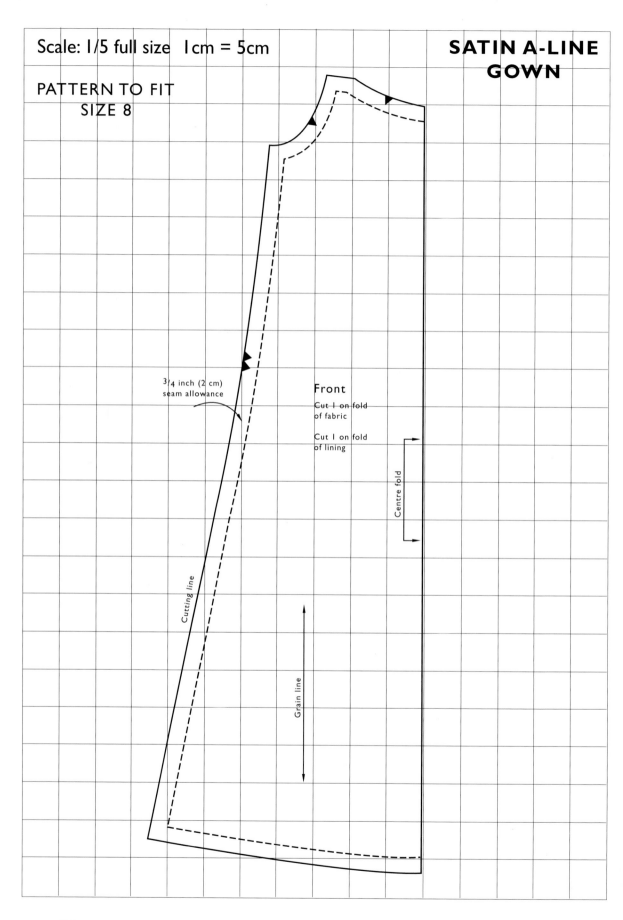

Scale: 1/5 full size 1cm = 5cm

**SATIN A-LINE
GOWN**

PATTERN TO FIT
SIZE 8

3/4 inch (2 cm)
seam allowance

Front

Cut 1 on fold
of fabric

Cut 1 on fold
of lining

Centre fold

Cutting line

Grain line

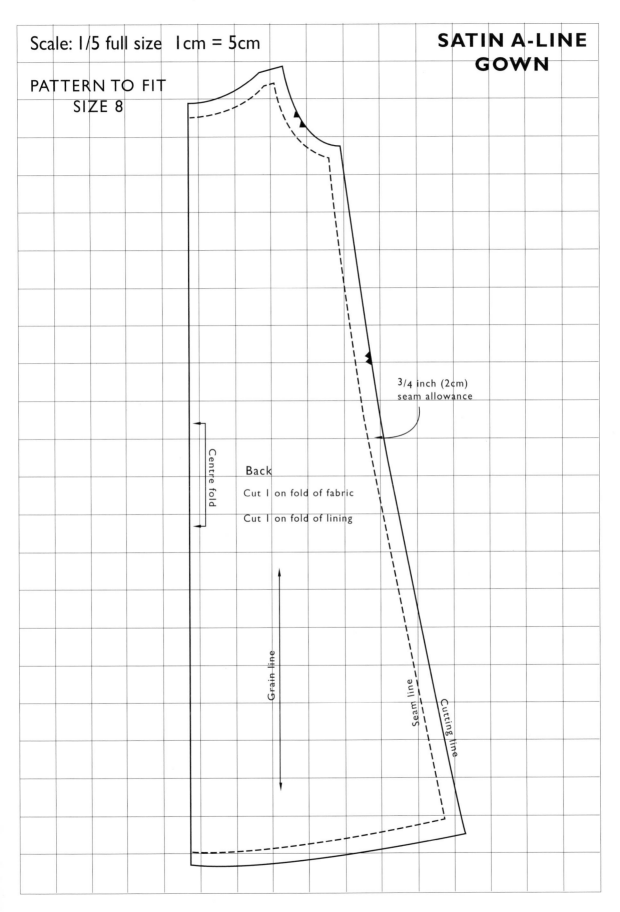

Scale: 1/5 full size 1cm = 5cm

SATIN A-LINE GOWN

PATTERN TO FIT
SIZE 8

3/4 inch (2cm)
seam allowance

Centre fold

Back

Cut 1 on fold of fabric

Cut 1 on fold of lining

Grain line

Seam line

Cutting line

Disco Top and Pants

This combination of top and pants in electric blue satin is a stunning outfit when dressed for the disco or a special party. The pattern also works well as a cool and comfortable garment for daywear when sewn in a bright soft cotton fabric.

Materials:

¾ yard (0.6 m) satin material, 45 inches (115 cm) wide for top
1 ¾ yards (1.5 m) satin material, 45 inches (115 cm) wide for pants
7 inch (18cm) zipper
reel of matching polyester thread.

Method:

TOP

1. Pin front to back at the sides right sides facing together matching nicks. Machine down to circles and leave openings.
2. Press seams open and overlock edges.
3. Fold each shoulder strap in half, right sides facing together. Machine a ½ inch (1.3 cm) seam. At the end insert a small safety pin and turn the strap out to the right side. Press straps.

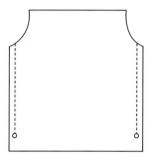

1. Machine front to back at side seams down to circles.

2. Fold each shoulder strap in half, machine along seam line. Turn right side out.

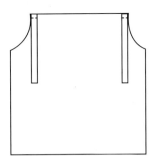

3. Pin straps to the right side of material at the back circles.

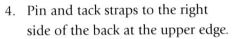

4. Pin and tack straps to the right side of the back at the upper edge.

5. Machine front and back facings at the side seams. Press seams flat open. Pin and tack facing to front and back of the top. Machine. Trim seams, cut away bulk diagonally at the corners.

6. Turn facing to the inside and press. Understitch as far as possible at the front and back. Overlock the raw edges of the facing.

7. Press up ¾ inch (2 cm) hem at the bottom of the top and machine a ½ inch (1.3 cm) seam along front and back of hem and around each opening at the sides.

8. Try the top on and adjust the back strap. Tack and stitch in place to the back of the top.

PANTS

1. Tack and machine darts in the back. Press darts towards the centre. Repeat with front darts.

2. Machine centre back seams and front seam. Overlock edges and press seams flat.

3. Tack and machine centre back to centre front, right sides facing

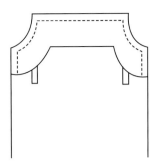

4. Machine front and back facings at side seams. Machine facing to front and back of the top.

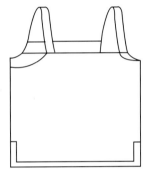

5. Handstitch the back straps in place. Press up the hem and machine around each side opening.

6. Machine darts in the front and the back. Machine centre back seam up to the circle.

together, matching inside leg
seams. Overlock edges. Press flat.

4. With front and back facing
   together at side seams, machine on
   left side below circle down to the
   opening slit section.

5. Machine right side of pants
   together from waistline down to
   split section. Overlock seams.

7. Machine in the zipper.

6. Set in zip in left side. (See instructions on page 36).

7. At the waistline and above the zip tack on the seam line for the exact waist
   position.

8. Cut a double self binding (see instructions on page 28) and tack and
   machine in the waist position.

9. On the right side of the pants and ½ inch (1.3 cm) from the waistline down
   machine a row of stitching.

10. Press up a ¾ inch (2 cm) hem at the bottom of the pants and machine a
    ½ inch (1.3 cm) seam along hem and around the leg openings.

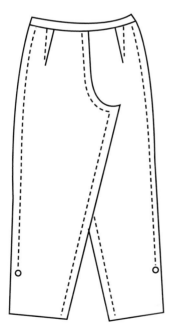

8. Machine centre front seam, and machine
   front and back at inside legs, and side
   seams down to circles. Machine a self
   binding on the waist line.

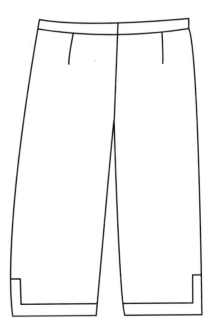

9. Machine a hem along hem of pants and
   around leg openings.

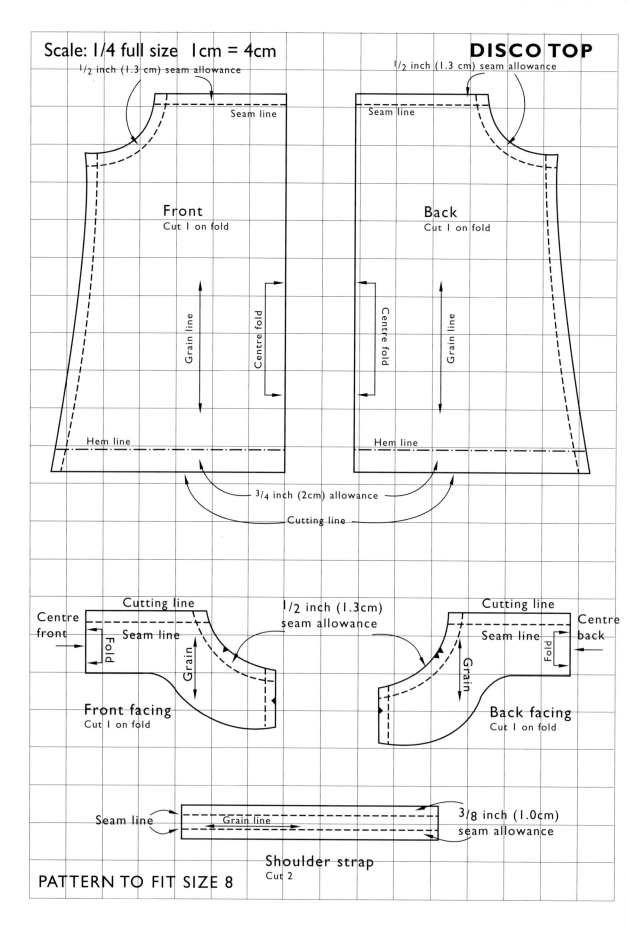

Scale: 1/4 full size 1cm = 4cm

DISCO TOP

1/2 inch (1.3 cm) seam allowance

1/2 inch (1.3 cm) seam allowance

Seam line

Seam line

Front
Cut 1 on fold

Back
Cut 1 on fold

Grain line

Centre fold

Centre fold

Grain line

Hem line

Hem line

3/4 inch (2cm) allowance

Cutting line

Cutting line

1/2 inch (1.3cm)
seam allowance

Cutting line

Centre
front

Centre
back

Seam line

Seam line

Fold

Fold

Grain

Grain

Front facing
Cut 1 on fold

Back facing
Cut 1 on fold

Seam line

Grain line

3/8 inch (1.0cm)
seam allowance

Shoulder strap
Cut 2

PATTERN TO FIT SIZE 8

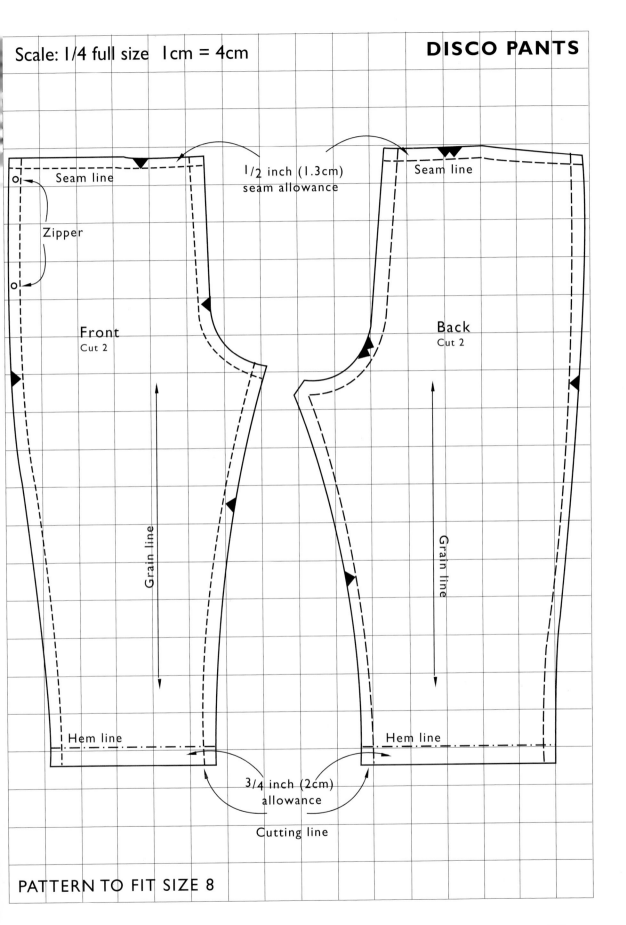

Seam line

1/2 inch (1.3cm)
seam allowance

Seam line

Zipper

Front
Cut 2

Back
Cut 2

Grain line

Grain line

Hem line

Hem line

3/4 inch (2cm)
allowance

Cutting line

PATTERN TO FIT SIZE 8

Velvet Gypsy Waistcoat

A velvet patchwork waistcoat over a peasant blouse and matched with a colourful brocade skirt is a stunning combination.

Materials:

¾ yard (0.6 m) velvet panne, 45 inches (115 cm) wide
1 ¾ yards (1.5 m) satin lining, 45 inches (115 cm) wide
matching polyester threads (for joining strips)
stretch machine needle (for sewing velvet)
4 x ¾ inch (2 cm) buttons

Method:

The amount of velvet material needed will depend on your colour coordination and size.

Cut velvet strips ¼ inch (6 cm) wide (½ inch/ 1.3cm allowance included) the length of your choice. With the stretch needle on your machine and using matching thread, join all strips into a square shape large enough to fit the two front sections.

1. On the wrong side of the square, pin the fronts lengthwise onto the fabric and cut.
2. On the wrong side of the satin, cut out two front sections. Also cut two back sections. *Note:* You have cut four front sections (two of velvet, two of lining) and two back sections of lining. Two front sections of fabric and one back section of lining will be used to make the waistcoat. The remaining front and back sections will be the waistcoat lining.

MACHINING THE WAISTCOAT

1. With right sides together machine the front to the back at the shoulder seams
2. Machine shoulder seams of lining. With right sides together, pin lining to the waistcoat and machine.

1. Right sides together machine front to back at shoulder seam.

78

3. Machine the lining to the waistcoat, leaving side seams open for turning. Trim the seams and corners, clip the curves.

4. Turn the waistcoat right side out by pulling each front through the shoulder and out of one of the back openings. Press.

5. With right sides together and raw edges even, pin the waistcoat and lining at the sides, matching armhole seams and lower seams.

6. To machine, begin on the lining 1 inch (2.5 cm) above the armhole seam. Machine waistcoat seam and end of lining 1 inch (2.5 cm) below the lower seam edge. Press seam open. Turn in seam allowances of remaining lining edges and slipstitch together.

7. Mark buttonhole placement on right front (with paper buttonhole guide). Lap fronts, matching the centres. Sew buttons under and in the centre of the buttonhole.

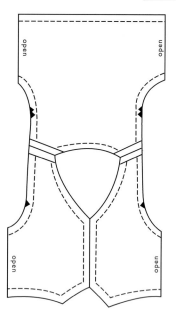

2. Machine shoulder seams of lining. Right sides together, tack lining to vest, matching shoulder seams. Machine lining to vest, leaving side seams open for turning.

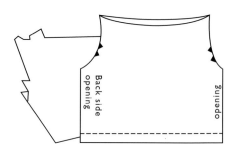

3. Turn vest right side out by pulling each front through shoulder and out one of the back side openings.

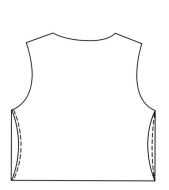

4. Right sides together, tack vest at sides and machine. Turn in seam allowance of remaining lining edges, and slipstitch together.

5. Machine buttonholes in the right front. Sew buttons in place in the centre of each buttonhole.

WAISTCOAT

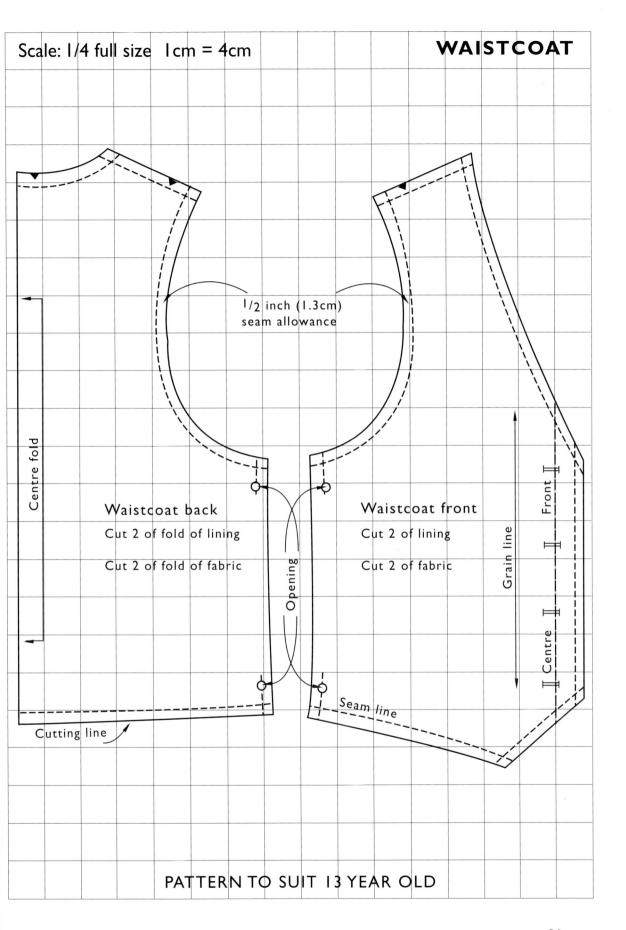

1/2 inch (1.3cm)
seam allowance

Centre fold

Waistcoat back

Cut 2 of fold of lining

Cut 2 of fold of fabric

Opening

Waistcoat front

Cut 2 of lining

Cut 2 of fabric

Grain line

Front

Centre

Seam line

Cutting line

PATTERN TO SUIT 13 YEAR OLD

Peasant Blouse

Materials:

1 ¾ yards (1.5 m) Broderie Anglaise, 45 inches (115 cm) wide

1 reel matching polyester thread

1 ½ yards (1 m) elastic ¼ inch (6 mm) wide.

Method:

1. With right sides facing, tack and machine the front and the back together at the side seams. Press seams towards the back and overlock the edges. Press towards the back.

2. Machine the sleeve seams facing together. Press and overlock the edges, press towards the back.

1. Tack. Machine front to back at side seams. Overlock edges. Press.

2. Tack and machine sleeve seam. Overlock edges and press.

3. With right sides together, pin sleeves to the armhole edge, matching underarm seams. Press seams up towards the top and overlock.

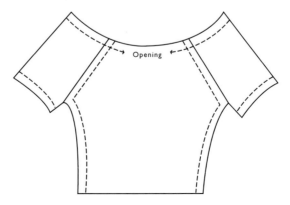

3. Tack and machine sleeve to armhole. Overlock edges. Press up a ⅝ inch (15 mm) hem line at the neck edge. Leave opening. Repeat on sleeve hems.

4. Press up ¾ inch (2 cm) all around the neckline to form a casing for the elastic, threading where the dots indicate.

5. At the hemline of the sleeves, press up a ¾ inch (2 cm) hem to form a casing. Machine close to the edge and leave an opening for the elastic, threading where the dots indicate.

6. Cut elastic, the measurement of the upper arm and allow and extra 1 inch (2.5cm). With a safety pin insert elastic through the opening, overlapping the ends. Hold with a safety pin. Try on and adjust to fit. Machine the ends of the elastic. Machine across the opening. Repeat this step to fit elastic into the neckline.

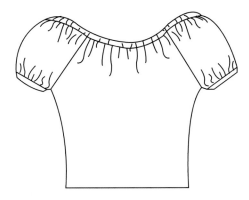

4. Press up a ⅝ inch (15 mm) hem on edge of blouse. Thread elastic through hem of sleeve openings, and neckline. Machine close the openings.

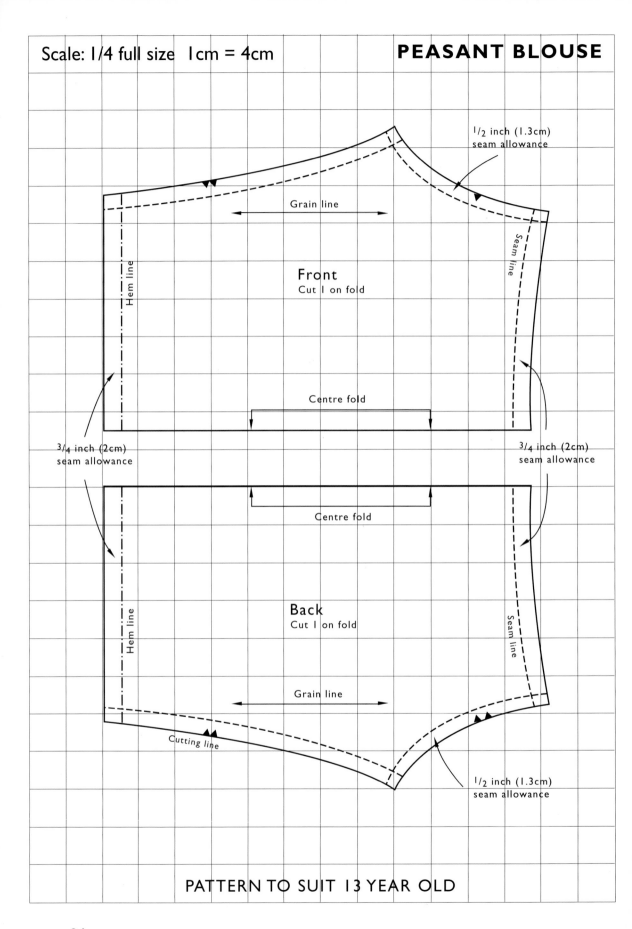

Scale: 1/4 full size 1cm = 4cm

PEASANT BLOUSE

1/2 inch (1.3cm) seam allowance

Grain line

Hem line

Seam line

Front
Cut 1 on fold

Centre fold

3/4 inch (2cm) seam allowance

3/4 inch (2cm) seam allowance

Centre fold

Hem line

Seam line

Back
Cut 1 on fold

Grain line

Cutting line

1/2 inch (1.3cm) seam allowance

PATTERN TO SUIT 13 YEAR OLD

Scale: 1/4 full size 1cm = 4cm

PEASANT BLOUSE

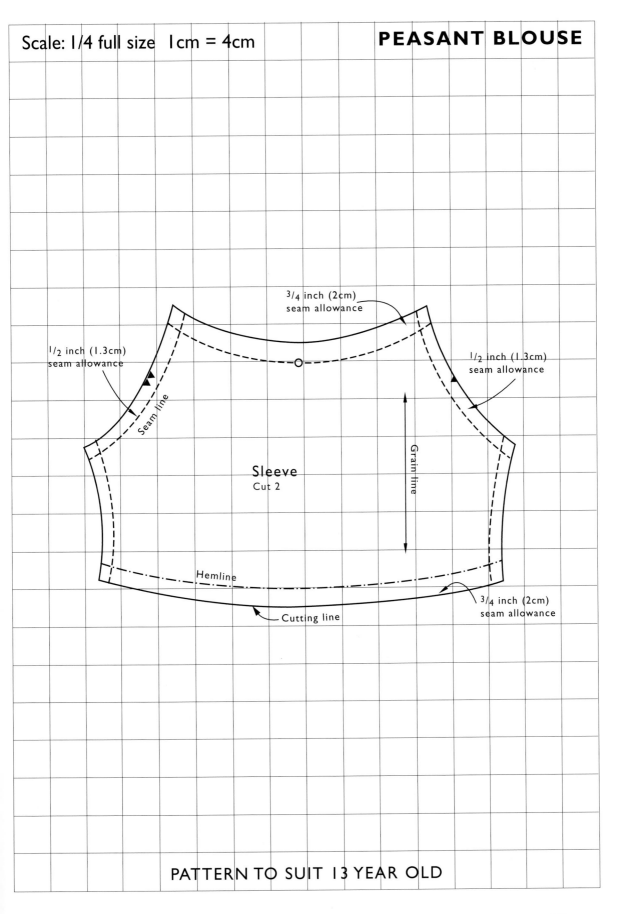

3/4 inch (2cm)
seam allowance

1/2 inch (1.3cm)
seam allowance

1/2 inch (1.3cm)
seam allowance

Seam line

Grain line

Sleeve
Cut 2

Hemline

Cutting line

3/4 inch (2cm)
seam allowance

PATTERN TO SUIT 13 YEAR OLD

Brocade Skirt

Materials:

  1 ½ yards (1.35 m) brocade material, 45 inches (115 cm) wide
  1 reel matching polyester thread
  1 ½ yards (1.2 m) black lace, 45 inches (115 cm) wide

Method:

1. Pin and tack the darts in the skirt back. Machine each dart from the upper edge towards the point. Tie off threads at the points. Press the darts toward the centre back.

2. With right side of back and front facing together, pin and tack side seams leaving left side above the circle open for zip. Press the seams flat open and overlock the edges.

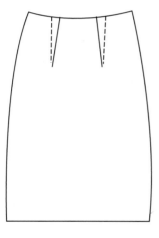 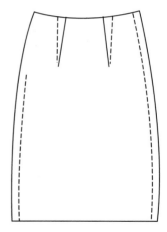

1. Tack and machine back darts. Press the darts towards the centre back.

2. Tack and machine side seams. Leave zipper opening on the left side. Overlock seams and press the seams open.

3. Set in the zip. (Refer to Setting in a Zip on page 36.)

4. Lay the front facing piece on the back facing piece so the right sides are together. Machine the right side seam to correspond to the skirt. Press the seam open, overlock the lower edge of the facing.

5. Tack the facing to the upper edge of the skirt with right sides facing and matching side seams. Turn under side edges of the facing at the zip side. Machine the upper edge of the facing to the skirt. Trim the seams and clip the curves.

6. Turn the facing to the inside. Tack the seam edge and press. Stitch the narrow edge to the zip by hand.

7. Overlock the bottom of the hem. Press up a ¾ inch (2 cm) hem. Measure lace around the hemline and make a ½ inch (1.3 cm) join. Pin join to one side of the skirt just underneath the hem edge. Tack in place and machine.

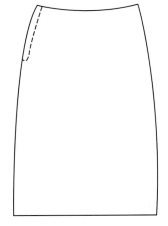

3. Tack and machine the zipper on the left side.

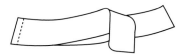

4. Joint the front facing seam, press seam open, overlock edge and overlock lower edge.

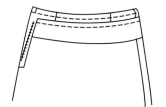

5. Tack and machine the facing to the upper edge of the skirt.

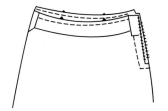

6. Turn the facing to the inside, handstitch the narrow edges of the facing near the zipper.

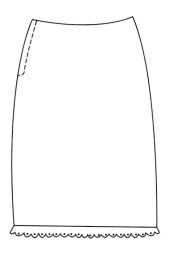

7. Press up ½ inch (13 mm) seam and overlock the edge, join seam of lace. Pin, tack and machine lace just under the hem line.

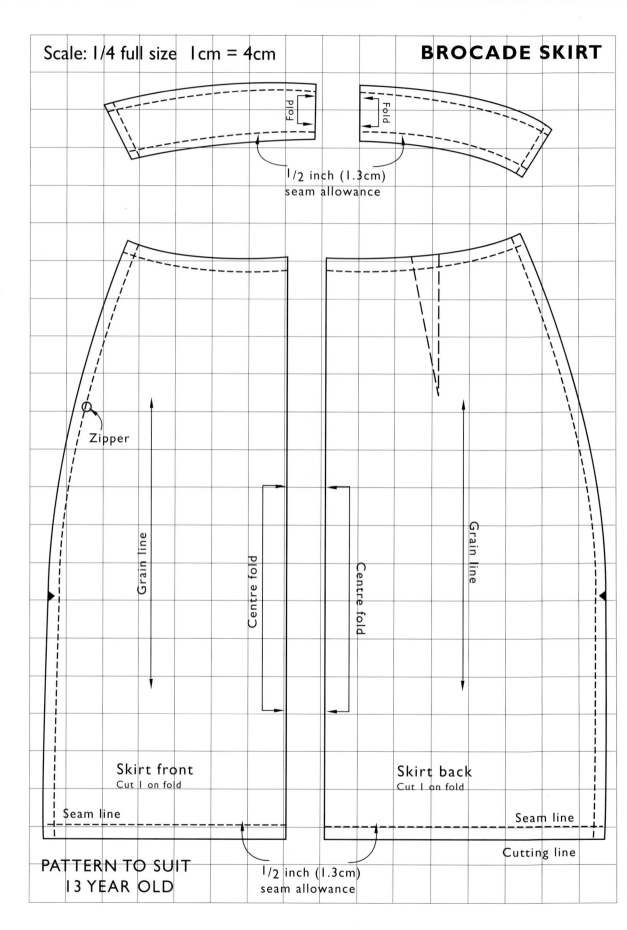

Scale: 1/4 full size   1cm = 4cm

BROCADE SKIRT

Fold

Fold

$1/2$ inch (1.3cm)
seam allowance

Zipper

Grain line

Centre fold

Centre fold

Grain line

Skirt front
Cut 1 on fold

Skirt back
Cut 1 on fold

Seam line

Seam line

Cutting line

PATTERN TO SUIT
13 YEAR OLD

$1/2$ inch (1.3cm)
seam allowance

Mandarin Jacket and Pedal Pushers

For something different to wear to that special occasion, this Mandarin Jacket and Pedal Pushers in Oriental print would look very chic.

Materials:

Top: 1 ⅝ yards (1.5 m) Oriental print cotton fabric, 45 inches (115 cm) wide

Pants: 1 ½ yards (1.4 m) fabric, 45 inches (115 cm) wide

large reel matching thread

1 inch (25 cm) iron on interfacing

elastic 8 inches (20 cm) long x 1 inch (2.5 cm) wide

4 buttons ½ inch (13 mm)

Method:

JACKET

1. Machine the front to the back at the shoulder seams, overlock edges and press towards the back.
2. Machine side seams down to openings, press seams open and overlock edges.

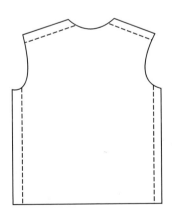

1. Machine front to back at shoulders.
Machine front to back at side seams.

3. With right sides together fold the underlap section in half lengthwise. Machine across the ends, trim the seams. Turn to the right side and press.

4. Pin and tack the underlap to the left front (matching nicks) and machine together.

5. Press interfacing to the wrong side of the collar. With right sides of collar together machine ⅝ inch (1.5 cm) from the notched edge of the collar.

6. Trim away the bulk and cut nicks in curved area, turn to the right side and press.

7. On the outside, pin the collar to the neck edge. Tack the collar to the front neck edge at nick sections.

8. With right sides together to the front neck edge. Clip neck edge through all thicknesses at the dots. Be careful not to catch in the free edge of the back collar. Clip curves and corners.

9. Turn the facing to the inside and press and tack the loose edge of the back neck seam. Machine close to the edge.

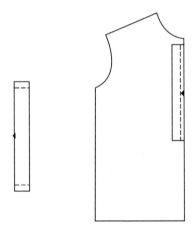

2. Machine underlap, press and turn to right side.
Machine underlap to left front matching nicks.

3. Machine collar sections together,
turn to right side (leaving notch edge
open between circles).

4. Pin collar to neck edge, be careful
not to catch in the free edge of the
back collar.

10. Tack and machine the seams of the sleeves, press flat open and overlock the edges. Press up a ¼ inch (6 mm) hem on the raw edge. Machine close to the edge.

11. Set in sleeves (Refer to setting in a sleeve on page 39)

12. Level the bottom of the jacket and press up a ¼ inch (6 mm) hem. Machine close to the edge.

13. On the right side measure the four buttonholes. (Use a paper buttonhole guide).

14. Bring the front edges together. Sew the buttons on the underlap.

5. Set in the sleeve. See instructions "Setting in a Sleeve" on page 39.

6. Press up ¼ inch (6 mm) hem at lower edge, machine close to the edge. On the right side measure the four buttonholes and machine. Sew the buttons in the centre on the underlap.

PANTS

1. Machine the centre back seam and front seam. Overlock edges and press seams flat.

2. Tack and machine centre back seam to centre front seam, right sides facing matching inside leg seams. Overlock edges. Press seams flat.

3. With front and back facing together machine down at the side seams. Overlock edges. Press towards the back.

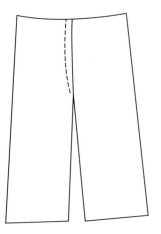

1. Machine centre front seam and back seam.

4. At the waistline press up a 1 ¼ inches (3.2 cm) hem to make a casing. Machine close to the lower edge of the casing leaving a 1 inch (2.5 cm) opening to insert the elastic.

5. Cut a piece of elastic to fit the waist allowing an extra 1 inch (2.5cm). Thread elastic through the casing and hold with a safety pin. Try the pants on and adjust the elastic to fit waistline. Machine overlap ends of elastic together, machine the opening closed.

6. Measure and level length of pants. Press up a ¾ inch (2 cm) hem, machine close to the pressed edge.

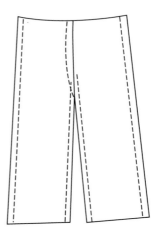

2. Machine back and front together at inside leg. Machine down side seams.

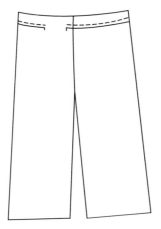

3. Machine the top hem line for the casing, leave opening for the elastic.

4. Thread elastic through casing, machine opening closed. Machine hem of pants legs.

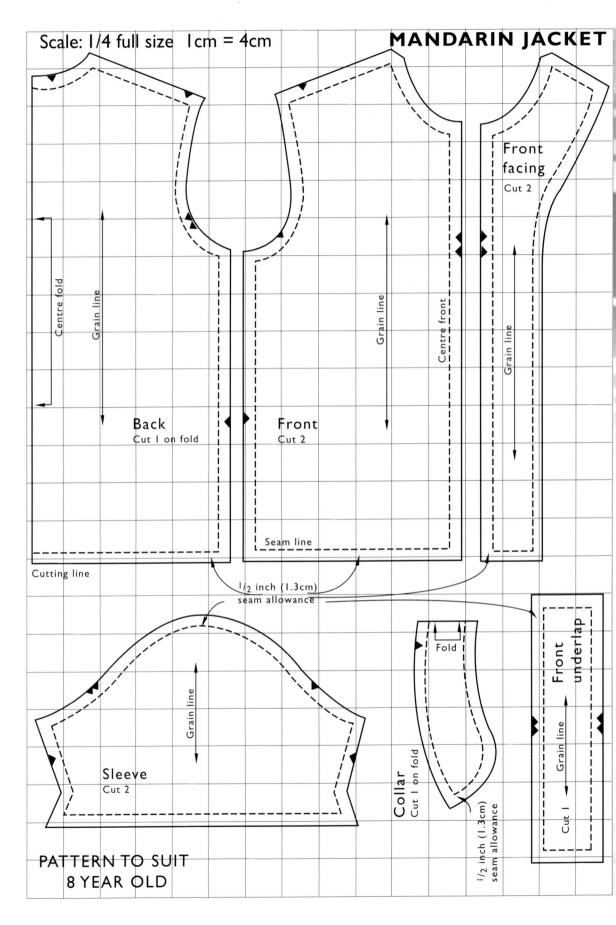

Scale: 1/4 full size 1cm = 4cm

MANDARIN JACKET

Front facing
Cut 2

Centre fold

Grain line

Grain line

Centre front

Grain line

Back
Cut 1 on fold

Front
Cut 2

Seam line

Cutting line

1/2 inch (1.3cm)
seam allowance

Fold

Front underlap

Sleeve
Cut 2

Grain line

Collar
Cut 1 on fold

Grain line

Cut 1

1/2 inch (1.3cm)
seam allowance

PATTERN TO SUIT
8 YEAR OLD

PEDAL PUSHERS

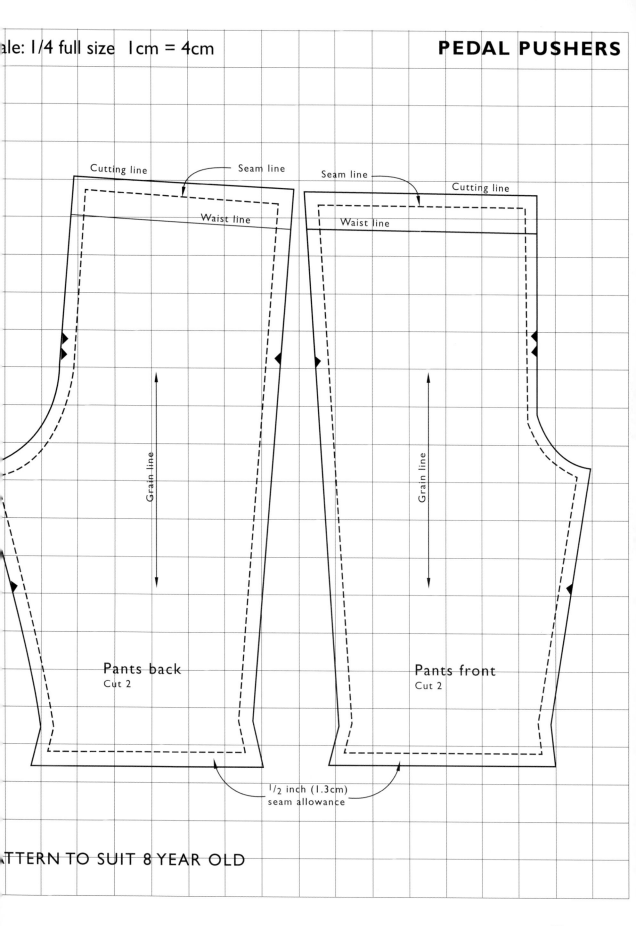

Cutting line

Seam line

Waist line

Seam line

Waist line

Cutting line

Grain line

Grain line

Pants back
Cut 2

Pants front
Cut 2

$^1/_2$ inch (1.3cm)
seam allowance

TTERN TO SUIT 8 YEAR OLD

Cargo Pants

These comfortable Cargo Pants can very quickly become a pair of shorts with the concealed attachment of strips of velcro. It is advisable before cutting out Cargo Pants in the fabric, to make a calico toile (Refer to Toile on page 16.) to accommodate adjustments to suit each individual.

Materials:

2 ¼ yards (2.1 m) drill material, 45 inches (115 cm) wide
matching polyester thread
1 card of ¾ inch (2 cm) wide elastic
4 inches (10 cm) 'Velcro' strips
1 metal hook and eye.

SHORTS SECTION OF CARGO PANTS
Method:

1. With right sides facing together, machine the centre seam in front between the nick and the circle.

SETTING IN THE FLY
FRONT ZIPPER

2. Back stitch ½ inch (1.3 cm) at the bottom of the zipper opening. (Attach a zipper foot to the machine.)

3. Press the extensions of the fly front under and along the fold lines on the pattern.

4. Place the closed zipper, facing up, under the folded edge, which forms the underlap.

1. Machine the centre seam in the front between the nick and the circle.

5. The fold should rest next to the zipper foot teeth. Tack to keep the zipper in position as you sew. Machine along the fold.

6. Tack the folded edge of the overlap to the zipper so it conceals the stitching.

7. Place the zipper facing up so that the only sections are under the zipper foot and the seam allowance of the overlap. Machine this zipper to this seam allowance as close as possible to the zipper teeth.

8. Machine a second row of stitching about ½ inch (3.2 cm) from the outer edge of the zipper.

9. Machine through all thicknesses of the garment from the right side along the stitching line on your pattern.

SIDE POCKETS

10. Machine pocket facing to the front, along the slanted edge. Right sides together, matching nicks. Trim seams.

11. Turn pocket facing to the front. Press. Edge machine finished edge of the fronts, machine again ¼ inch (6 mm) from front stitching.

12. Machine front inset and pocket facing, right sides together. Press seam edges together and overlock. Tack across upper and side edges.

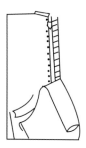

2. Press the extensions along the fold lines. Tack in the closed zipper facing up.

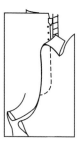

3. Tack the folded edge of the overlap to conceal stitching and machine through all thicknesses from the right side along the stitching line on the pattern.

4. Machine pocket facing to the front along slanted edge.

5. Machine front inset and pocket facing, right sides together.

13. Press ¼ inch (6 mm) on long un-nicked edge of waistband, and machine. Trim seams and press seam allowance towards the waistband.

14. Open the zipper, pin and tack waistband to the pants, right sides together and machine.

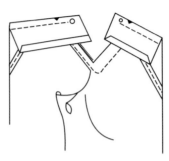

6. Open zipper, pin waistband to pants.

15. Machine centre seam of the back from upper edge to nicks.

16. To sew casing, turn down ½ inch (1.3 cm) on upper edge of back. Press.

17. Turn under ¼ inch (6 mm) on raw edge and machine in place. Machine again ¼ inch (6 mm) above first stitching.

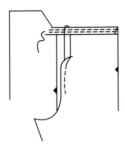

7. Turn down 1 ¼ inch (3.2 cm) seam to make a casing for elastic on the upper edge of the back.

18. Cut two pieces of elastic 18 inches (0.5 m). Thread elastic through casings, pin, tack and machine across ends. Trim bulk from elastic ends.

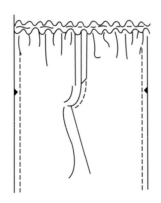

8. Insert elastic through casing. Machine across ends, right sides facing. Machine front to back at both sides.

19. With right sides together, pin, tack and machine front to back at the sides and upper edge of back at the fold line on the waistband.

20. Clip back seam allowance below the casing. Press side seams open below the clip.

FRONT FLAP POCKETS

21. Fold each pocket on the solid line, right sides together, matching the circles. Machine along dotted lines from upper and lower edge to the circle. Tack along the dotted line between the circles.

22. To form pleats on the inside, bring fold to stitching. Press, tack across the pleat.

23. Turn the pocket to the inside, press up a ¾ inch (20 mm) hem at the top of the pocket (cut off bulk diagonally at the corners) and machine close to the edge.

24. Cut two 1 inch (2.5 cm) pieces of Velcro, position in place on the top of the pocket on the right side where indicated on the pattern, machine all around the edge.

25. Press seams of sides and lower edge of the pockets and edge stitch. Pin pockets in position on each front and back. Edge stitch, machine again ¼ inch (6 mm) from first stitching.

26. With right sides of flaps facing together, pin and tack and machine stitch sides and lower edge together. Cut off bulk diagonally at the corners.

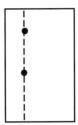

9. Fold each pocket on the solid line. Machine along dotted line.

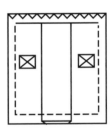

10. To form pleat bring fold to stitching. Machine velcro squares in place.

11. Right sides facing, machine flap. Turn to right side.

27. Turn right side out. Press and overlock raw edges together.

28. Edge stitch finished edges of the flaps. Machine again ¼ inch (6 mm) from first stitching.

29. Cut two matching 1 inch (2.5 cm) pieces of Velcro to join together the other two pieces, position it on the wrong side of the flaps and machine all the way around. On the right side of the Velcro squares top machine diagonally from corner to corner.

30. With right sides together, pin flap on each front and back with raw edges of flap extending 1 ¼ inches (3.2 cm) below placement line. Machine ¼ inch (6 mm) from raw edges.

31. Machine from front to back at inside leg edges, right sides together matching nicks, overlock seams and press.

32. Fold waistband on the fold lines wrong sides together. Machine the pressed under edges of the waistband over the seam and ends of back casing. Press and machine ¼ inch (6 mm) away from first stitching.

33. Hand stitch hook and eye to the edge of the waistband.

34. Press up 1 ¼ inches (3.2 cm) hem at the bottom of shorts, overlock the edges. Tack and machine a strip of Velcro on the inside of the hem line.

12. Machine velcro squares to flaps.

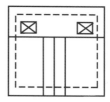

13. Pocket ready to sew to pants.

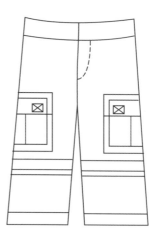

14. Machine pockets on placement line to pants. Machine pants side seams. Machine hem on pants. Stitch metal hook to waist line flap.

REMOVABLE LEG SECTION OF CARGO PANTS

35. With right sides of lower leg section facing, machine side seams, overlock the edges and press flat. Turn to the right side. Overlock the top. Tack and machine other side of Velcro strip 1 inch (2.5 cm) below the top overlocking and on the right side and in line with the shorts section.

36. Press up a 1 ¼ inches (3.2 cm) hem and machine at the bottom of the removable legs.

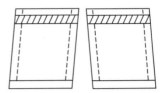

15. Machine lower leg section down side seams on the right side. Machine velcro on line. Machine hems of pants.

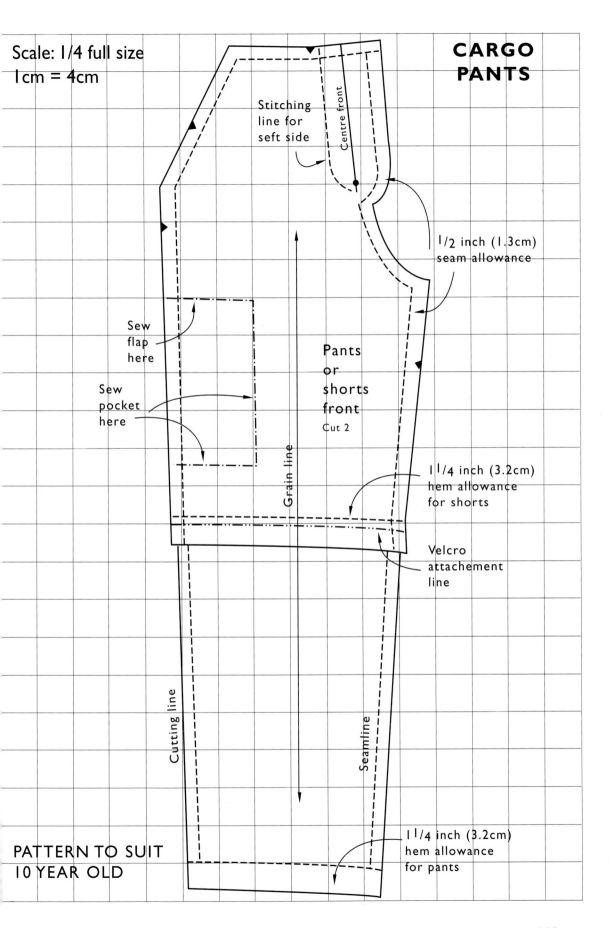

Scale: 1/4 full size
1cm = 4cm

CARGO PANTS

Stitching line for seft side

Centre front

1/2 inch (1.3cm) seam allowance

Sew flap here

Sew pocket here

Pants or shorts front
Cut 2

Grain line

1 1/4 inch (3.2cm) hem allowance for shorts

Velcro attachement line

Cutting line

Seamline

1 1/4 inch (3.2cm) hem allowance for pants

PATTERN TO SUIT 10 YEAR OLD

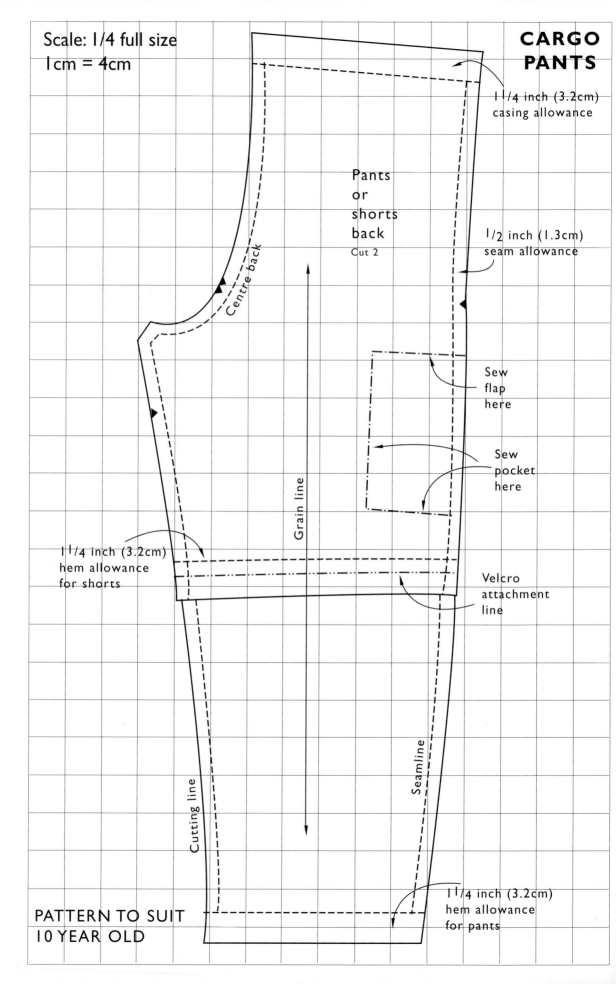

Scale: 1/4 full size
1cm = 4cm

CARGO PANTS

1 1/4 inch (3.2cm) casing allowance

Pants or shorts back
Cut 2

1/2 inch (1.3cm) seam allowance

Centre back

Sew flap here

Sew pocket here

Grain line

1 1/4 inch (3.2cm) hem allowance for shorts

Velcro attachment line

Cutting line

Seamline

1 1/4 inch (3.2cm) hem allowance for pants

PATTERN TO SUIT
10 YEAR OLD

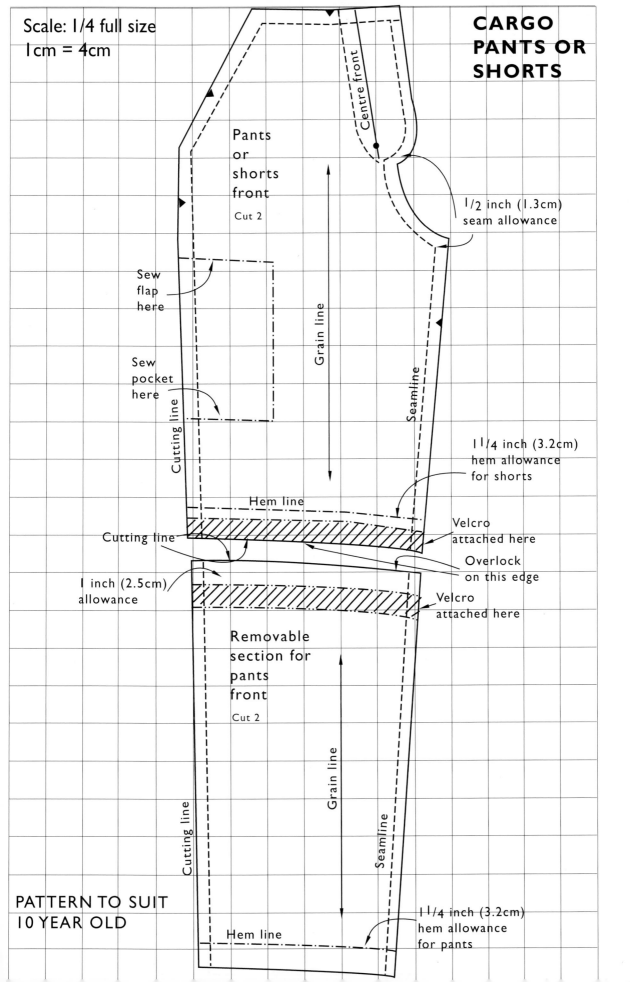

Scale: 1/4 full size

1cm = 4cm

CARGO PANTS OR SHORTS

Pants or shorts front

Cut 2

Centre front

1/2 inch (1.3cm) seam allowance

Sew flap here

Sew pocket here

Cutting line

Grain line

Seamline

1 1/4 inch (3.2cm) hem allowance for shorts

Hem line

Cutting line

Velcro attached here

Overlock on this edge

1 inch (2.5cm) allowance

Velcro attached here

Removable section for pants front

Cut 2

Grain line

Seamline

Cutting line

Hem line

1 1/4 inch (3.2cm) hem allowance for pants

PATTERN TO SUIT 10 YEAR OLD

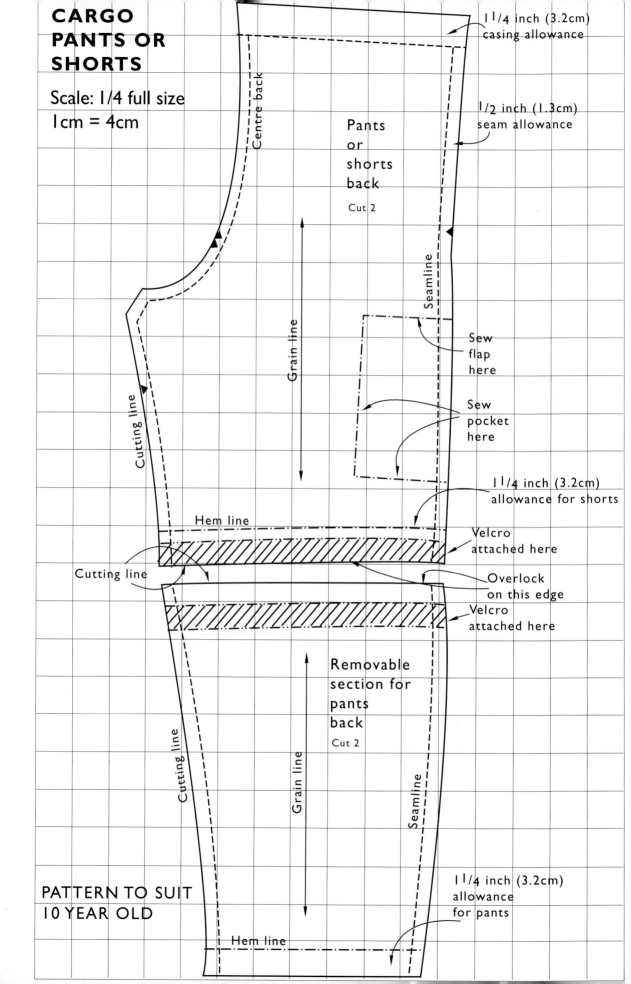

CARGO PANTS OR SHORTS

Scale: 1/4 full size
1cm = 4cm

Centre back

Pants
or
shorts
back

Cut 2

Grain line

Cutting line

Hem line

Cutting line

1 1/4 inch (3.2cm) casing allowance

1/2 inch (1.3cm) seam allowance

Seamline

Sew flap here

Sew pocket here

1 1/4 inch (3.2cm) allowance for shorts

Velcro attached here

Overlock on this edge

Velcro attached here

Removable section for pants back

Cut 2

Grain line

Cutting line

Seamline

1 1/4 inch (3.2cm) allowance for pants

PATTERN TO SUIT
10 YEAR OLD

Hem line

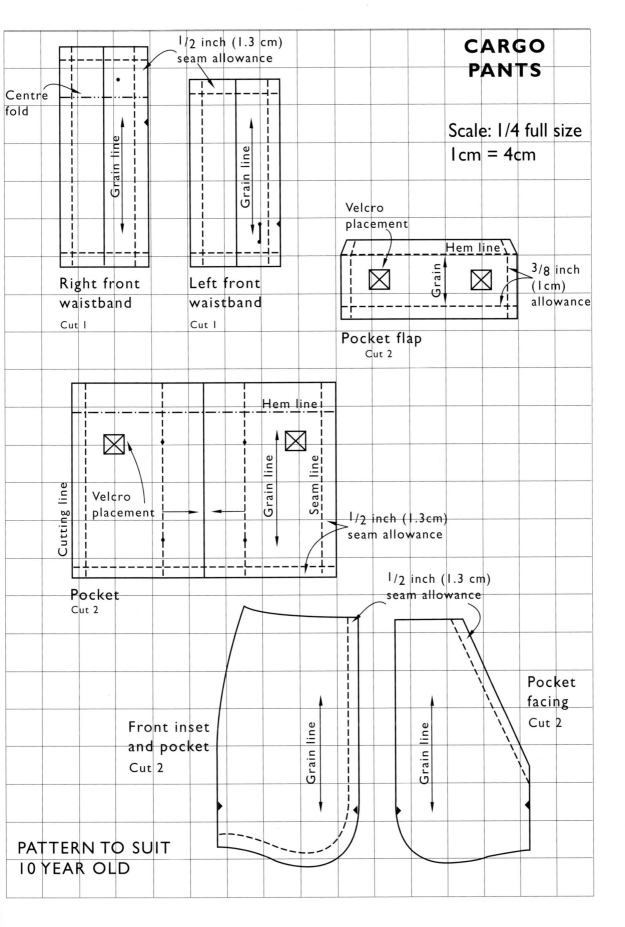

Centre fold

1/2 inch (1.3 cm) seam allowance

CARGO PANTS

Scale: 1/4 full size
1 cm = 4 cm

Grain line

Grain line

Right front waistband
Cut 1

Left front waistband
Cut 1

Velcro placement

Hem line

Grain

3/8 inch (1 cm) allowance

Pocket flap
Cut 2

Hem line

Cutting line

Velcro placement

Grain line

Seam line

1/2 inch (1.3cm) seam allowance

Pocket
Cut 2

1/2 inch (1.3 cm) seam allowance

1/2 inch (1.3 cm) seam allowance

Pocket facing
Cut 2

Front inset and pocket
Cut 2

Grain line

Grain line

PATTERN TO SUIT 10 YEAR OLD

Boys' Shirt

This shirt is modern, cool and comfortable to wear and looks great teamed with cargo pants or shorts.

Materials:

1 ¾ yards (1.5 m) cotton and polyester fabric, 45 inches (115 cm) wide
one reel matching polyester thread
4 matching ¾ inch (2 cm) buttons
¼ yard (0.25 m) interfacing

Method:

1. With right sides facing pin back to front at shoulders, overlock seams and press towards the back.

1. Machine back to front at shoulders

2. Press ½ inch (1.3 cm) on upper edge of pocket. Turn pocket to outside on hemline, cut off bulk at corners.

2. Machine pocket

3. Turn hem to inside, press under ¼ inch (6 mm) on sides, fold in corners, machine hem in place. Pin pocket on left shirt front on placement line — tack and machine sides and lower edge of pocket.

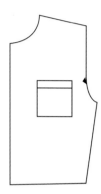

3. Position and machine pocket on placement line on left front.

4. Baste interfacing to wrong side of the collar, tack and machine the two collars facing together — cut bulk away from corners, turn to right side and press flat.

4. Machine collar. Turn to right side.

5. Pin collar to neck edge, right side up (matching nicks and centre backs).
6. Make a ¼ inch (6 mm) clip on upper layer of collar at circles.
7. Unpin upper layer of collar between clips. Tack collar to the neck edge, keeping upper layer free between clips and clipping neck curve as needed.
8. Press under ¼ inch (6 mm) on shoulder edges of front facing. Turn facings to outside on facing line (over-collar) matching nicks. Pin and tack neck edge keeping upper layer of collar free between clips. Cut bulk off at corners, clip curves. Press.
9. Turn facing to inside, folding fronts on facing lines. Press neck seam allowances in the back towards the collar. Turn under ¼ inch (6 mm) on free edge of collar and top machine over seam.

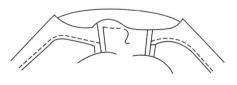

5. Machine collar to neck edge.

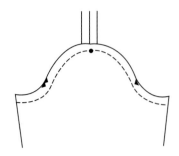

6. Machine sleeves in armholes.

10. Set in sleeves (refer to Setting in a Shirt Sleeve on page 39)
11. Pin underarm seam of shirt and sleeve matching nicks. Machine from sleeve shirt to hemline. Overlock seams and press seams towards the back.

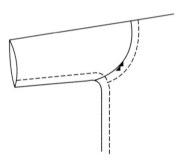

7. Machine underarm of shirt and sleeve.

12. Press up a ¾ inch (2 cm) hem on lower edge of sleeve, press and machine.
13. Press up a ¾ inch (2 cm) hem on lower edge of shirt and machine close to the edge.
14. Machine buttonholes in the left front at markings. Sew a button in the centre of each buttonhole.

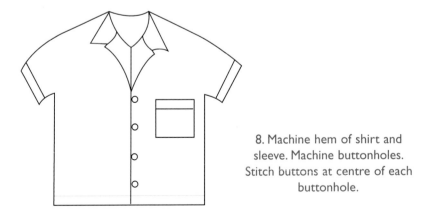

8. Machine hem of shirt and sleeve. Machine buttonholes. Stitch buttons at centre of each buttonhole.

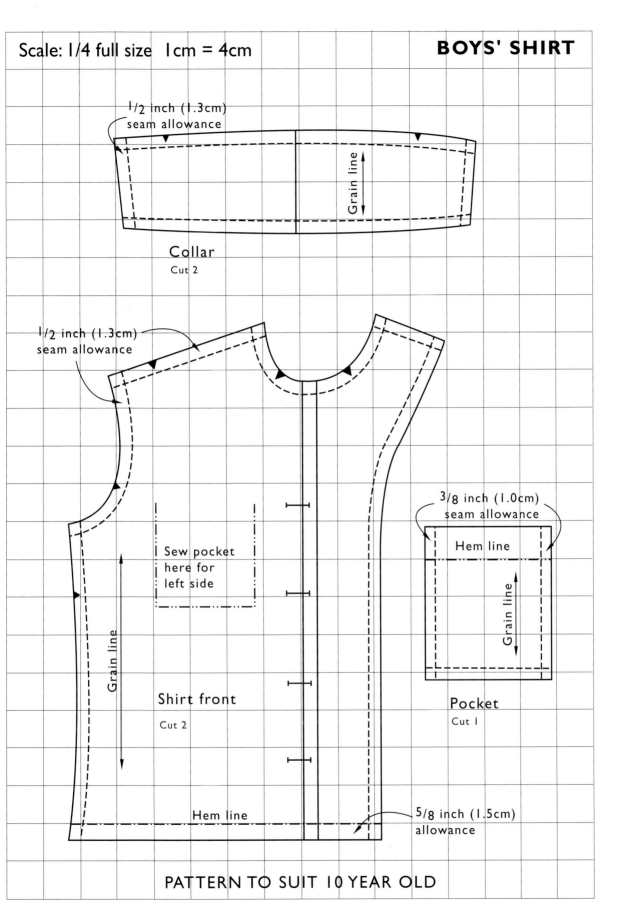

Scale: 1/4 full size   1cm = 4cm

BOYS' SHIRT

1/2 inch (1.3cm)
seam allowance

Grain line

Collar
Cut 2

1/2 inch (1.3cm)
seam allowance

Grain line

Sew pocket
here for
left side

Shirt front
Cut 2

Hem line

3/8 inch (1.0cm)
seam allowance

Hem line

Grain line

Pocket
Cut 1

5/8 inch (1.5cm)
allowance

PATTERN TO SUIT 10 YEAR OLD

Scale: 1/4 full size

1cm = 4cm

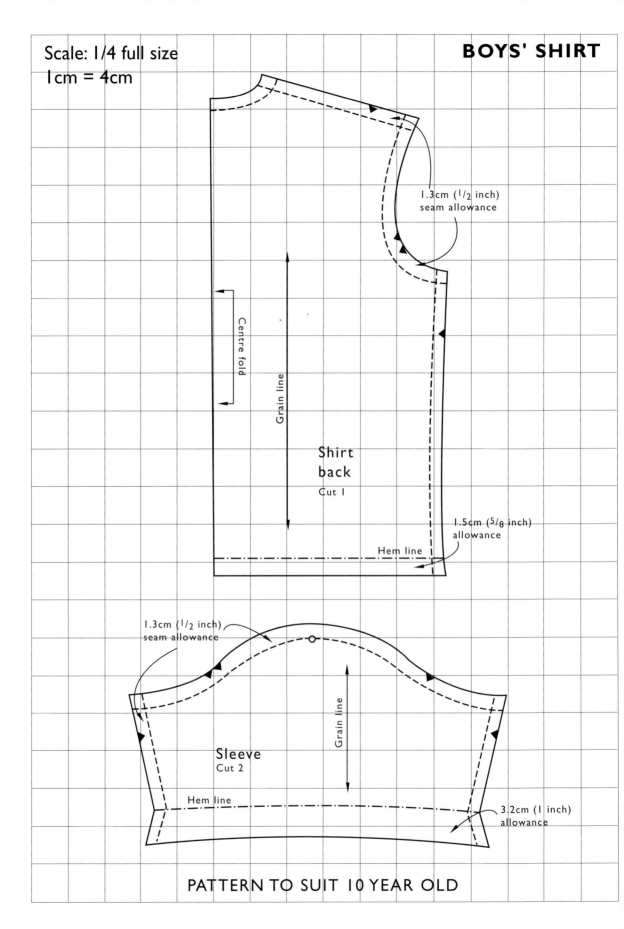

1.3cm (1/2 inch)
seam allowance

Centre fold

Grain line

Shirt
back
Cut 1

1.5cm (5/8 inch)
allowance

Hem line

1.3cm (1/2 inch)
seam allowance

Grain line

Sleeve
Cut 2

Hem line

3.2cm (1 inch)
allowance

PATTERN TO SUIT 10 YEAR OLD

Boys' Pyjamas

These warm, cosy pyjamas are so comfortable to wear tucked up in bed on a cold, winter night.

Materials:

    3 ½ yards (3.1 m) fabric, 45 inches (115 cm) wide

    matching polyester thread

    ¾ yard (0.7 m) elastic 1 inch (2.5cm) wide

    4 x ¾ inch (2 cm) buttons.

Method:

COAT

1. With the right side of front and back facing together, pin, tack and machine shoulder seams, overlock edges and press seam towards the back.
2. Pin, tack and machine front facing to the back neck facing. Press seams towards the back.
3. With right sides of front and back facing and matching the shoulder seams and the nicks, pin and tack around the neck edge and down the two fronts. Press seam towards the inside and understitch close to the edge. Overlock the raw edge of the facing.

1. Machine back to front at shoulders

2. Machine shoulder seams of facing. Machine facing all around the neckline.

4. With right sides together, pin sleeve to the armhole edge matching nicks, underarm edges and sleeve circle to the shoulder seam. Tack and machine, trim seam and press seam allowances toward sleeve and pants.

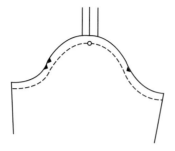

3. Machine sleeves to armhole edges.

5. Pin underarm seam of the top and sleeve, matching armhole seams, nicks and circles. Machine from sleeve edge down to the hemline. Press seam towards the back and overlock edges.

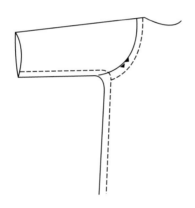

4. Machine underarm edges of jacket and sleeves. Machine pocket in place.

6. Press up ⅞ inch (2.2 cm) hem on sleeves and machine close to the edge.
7. Level the bottom hemline and press up a ⅞ inch (2.2 cm) hem. Machine close to the edge.
8. Make buttonholes in the left front at markings and sew buttons underneath and in the centre of the buttonholes.

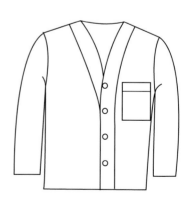

5. Machine hem of jacket and sleeves. Machine button holes. Stitch button in centre of each buttonhole.

PANTS

1. Machine centre back seam and front seam, overlock edges and press seams flat.

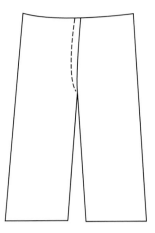

1. Machine centre back seam and machine centre front seam.

2. Tack and machine centre back seam to centre front seam, right sides facing matching inside leg seams and overlock edges. Press seams flat.
3. With front and back facing together, machine down at the side seams. Overlock edges and press towards the back.

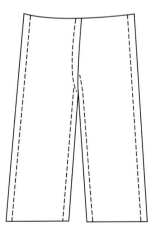

2. Machine back and front together at inside leg. Machine down side seams.

4. At the waist line press up a 1 ¼ inches (3.2 cm) hem to make a casing. Leave a 1 ⅛ inch (2.75 cm) opening to insert elastic.

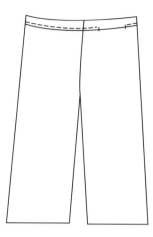

3. Machine the top hem line for the casing.
Leave opening for elastic.

5. Cut a piece of elastic to fit the waist plus 1 inch (2.5 cm). Thread elastic through the casing and hold with a safety pin. Try on the pants and adjust elastic to fit the waistline. Machine overlapping edges of elastic together, machine opening closed.
6. Measure and level length of pants, press up a ¾ inch (2 cm) hem, machine close to the pressed edge.

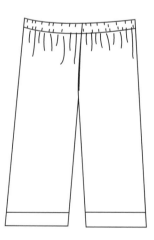

4. Thread elastic through casing. Machine
opening closed. Machine hem of pants legs.

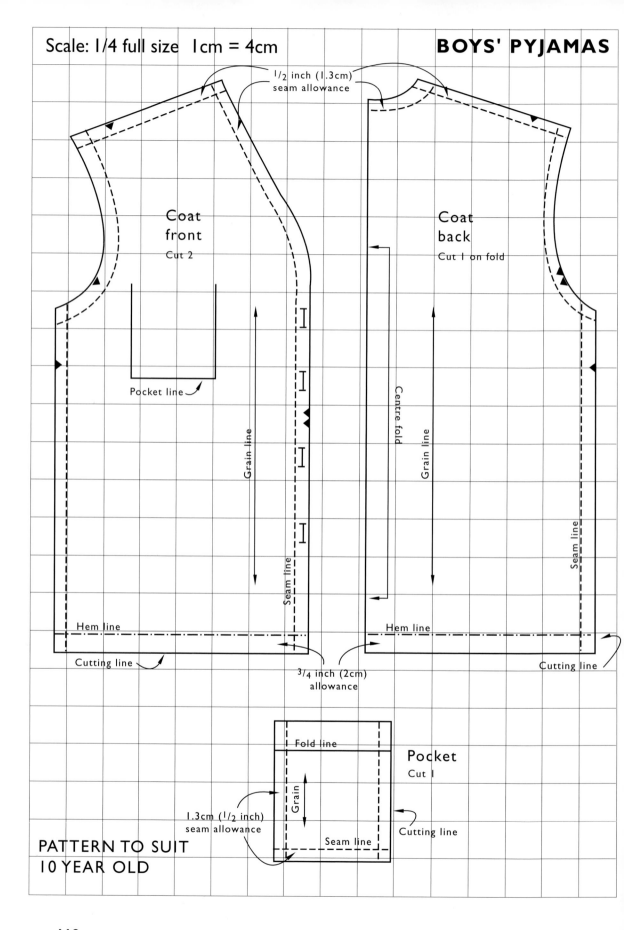

Scale: 1/4 full size   1cm = 4cm

BOYS' PYJAMAS

1/2 inch (1.3cm)
seam allowance

Coat
front
Cut 2

Coat
back
Cut 1 on fold

Pocket line

Grain line

Centre fold

Grain line

Seam line

Seam line

Hem line

Hem line

Cutting line

Cutting line

3/4 inch (2cm)
allowance

Fold line

Pocket
Cut 1

Grain

1.3cm (1/2 inch)
seam allowance

Seam line

Cutting line

PATTERN TO SUIT
10 YEAR OLD

BOYS' PYJAMAS

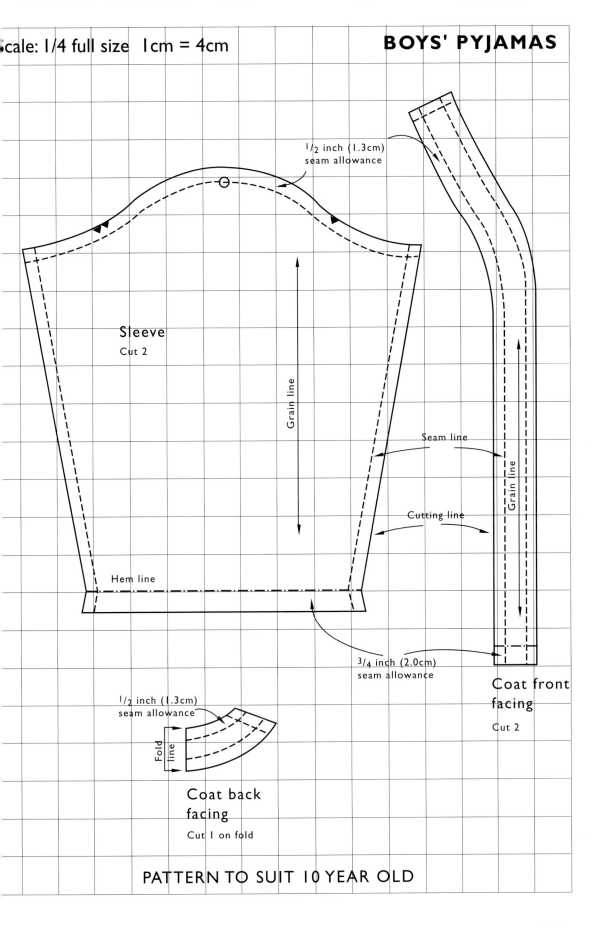

1/2 inch (1.3cm)
seam allowance

Sleeve
Cut 2

Grain line

Seam line

Grain line

Cutting line

Hem line

3/4 inch (2.0cm)
seam allowance

Coat front
facing

Cut 2

1/2 inch (1.3cm)
seam allowance

Fold line

Coat back
facing

Cut 1 on fold

PATTERN TO SUIT 10 YEAR OLD

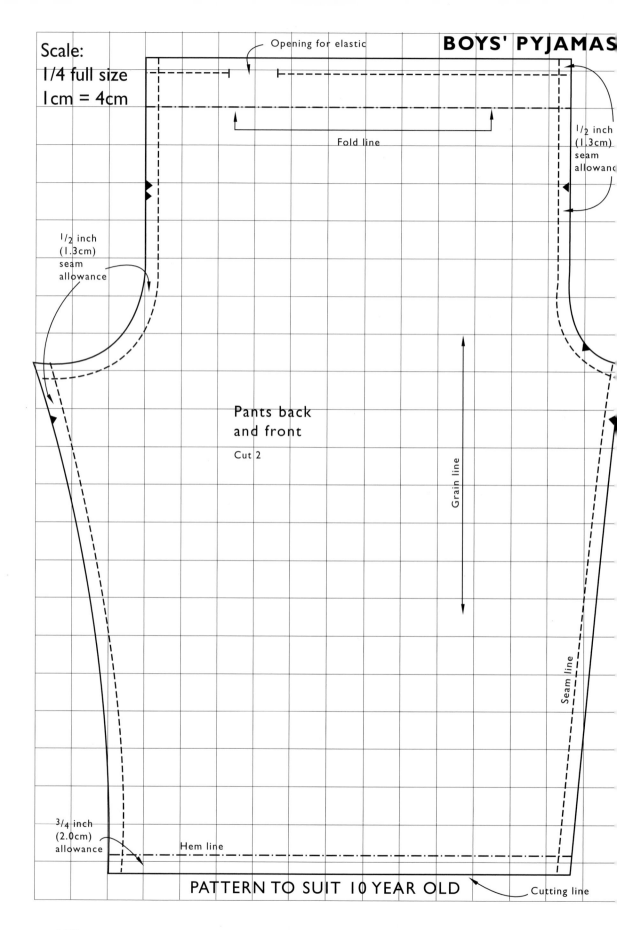

Scale:
1/4 full size
1cm = 4cm

Opening for elastic

BOYS' PYJAMAS

1/2 inch (1.3cm) seam allowance

Fold line

1/2 inch (1.3cm) seam allowance

Pants back and front

Cut 2

Grain line

Seam line

3/4 inch (2.0cm) allowance

Hem line

PATTERN TO SUIT 10 YEAR OLD

Cutting line

Accessories

Flower Embroidered Hat

This summer straw hat with the large embroidered daisy in silk ribbon will add a touch of glamour whenever you wear it.

Materials:

Straw hat
one card green silk ribbon ¼ inch (6 mm) wide
one card pink silk ribbon ¼ inch (6 mm) wide
one card brown silk ribbon ¼ inch (6 mm) wide
tapestry needle

Method:

1. Mark the centre of the crown of the hat, and decide how large you want the daisy flower and how many petals. Leave a tiny centre area to sew a group of French knots. The lazy daisy and leaves are chain stitch.
2. Bring the ribbon up through the hole in the weave of the hat. Hold it down with your thumb and insert the needle again at the starting point. Bring it out a short distance away, making sure the needle comes over the thread. Now take a small holding stitch at the top of the loop.
3. Thread the needle with the green silk ribbon to sew the leaves between the pink petals.

FRENCH KNOTS

1. Thread the needle with the brown silk ribbon.
2. Bring the needle through the centre of the flower, twist it (once only) around the needle then insert the needle into the straw close to the starting point and pull through to the back. Hold the thread firmly with the left thumb while pulling the thread through.
3. Fill up the centre with remaining French knots.

Kerchief

The triangular kerchief is a flattering modern accessory and can be sewn in different fabrics including lace and velvet.

Materials:

1 yard (1 m) material of your choice
one card matching bias binding
1 reel matching polyester thread.

Method:

1. Lay the pattern on the bias of the fabric. (See page 27 for cutting on the bias.)
2. With the right side of the scarf and the bias binding facing and open — pin, tack and machine from point A to B to C. Press and bring the other side of the bias over the seam and machine close to the edge and press.
3. Cut a length of binding and allow 9 inches (23 cm) at each end from A to C for a tie at the back. Repeat, stitching the same as step 2. Tie a knot at each end of the ties.

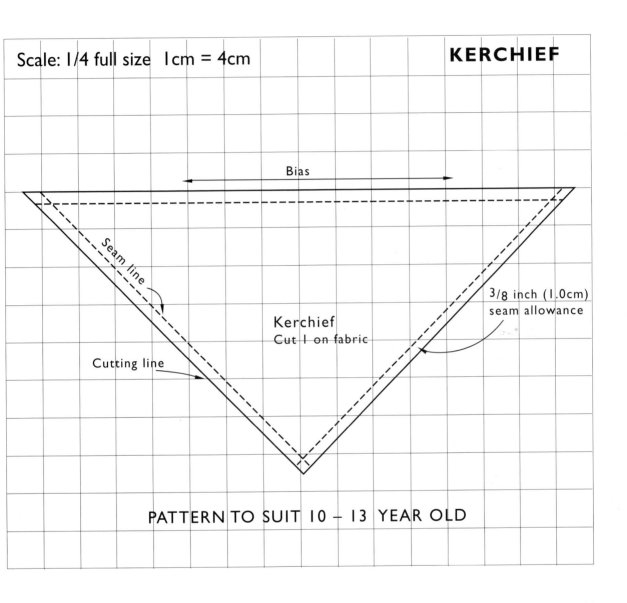

Scale: 1/4 full size 1cm = 4cm

KERCHIEF

Bias

Seam line

3/8 inch (1.0cm)
seam allowance

Kerchief
Cut 1 on fabric

Cutting line

PATTERN TO SUIT 10 – 13 YEAR OLD

Knitted Kerchief

The hand knitted woollen kerchief is a warm and practical accessory to wear with matching garments.

Materials:

1 ball 8 ply wool
stitch holder
one pair No. 7 (4.5 mm) knitting needles.

Method:

1. Cast on one stitch. Increase at each end of the row until it measures 8 inches (20.5 cm) long.
2. Knit 6 stitches and thread onto a stitch holder.
3. Cast off remaining stitches and leave another 6 at the end.
4. Knit the 6 stitches 4 inches (10cm) long and cast off.
5. Pick up the remaining 6 stitches on the stitch holder, tie the wool on and knit 4 inches (10cm) long, to match the other side for the ties at the back.

Beaded Beret

Stitching coloured beads on the brim of a black beret and adding a black tassel at the back looks very chic.

Materials:
black tassel
black beret
packet coloured glass beads of your choice
bead needle
beading thread.

Method:
1. Stitch, with a double black thread, the tassel to the centre of the top of the beret.
2. Thread the bead needle with a double beading thread.
3. Group the beads into a flower pattern to the front of the beret (of your own selection).

Fur Fabric Muff

Little girls feel very special and grown up if they can carry their own special muff.

Materials:

12 inches (28 cm) fur fabric
12 inches (28 cm) matching taffeta (lining)
matching polyester thread
18 inches (½ m) of quilting wadding
1 yard (1 m) black cording (for neck tie) — optional

Method:

1. With pattern, cut one of fur fabric, one of quilting wadding and one of taffeta.
2. Baste the wadding to the wrong side of the fur fabric. (Treat this now as one material.)
3. With right side of fur fabric and lining facing, machine down each side from top circle to bottom circle. Trim the seam and turn to the right side. Press the seam with a pressing cloth and a warm iron (not steam).
4. Machine the top seam of the fur fabric right across. Press the seam flat holding a pad underneath.
5. At the two top raw seam of the lining, press the seam allowance under and hand stitch across, also hand stitch each side at the top. Turn the muff to the right side.
6. If using the neck cord, measure the length and thread through the muff and tie a knot. Keep knot join inside the muff.

Scale: 1/4 full size 1cm = 4cm

FUR FABRIC MUFF

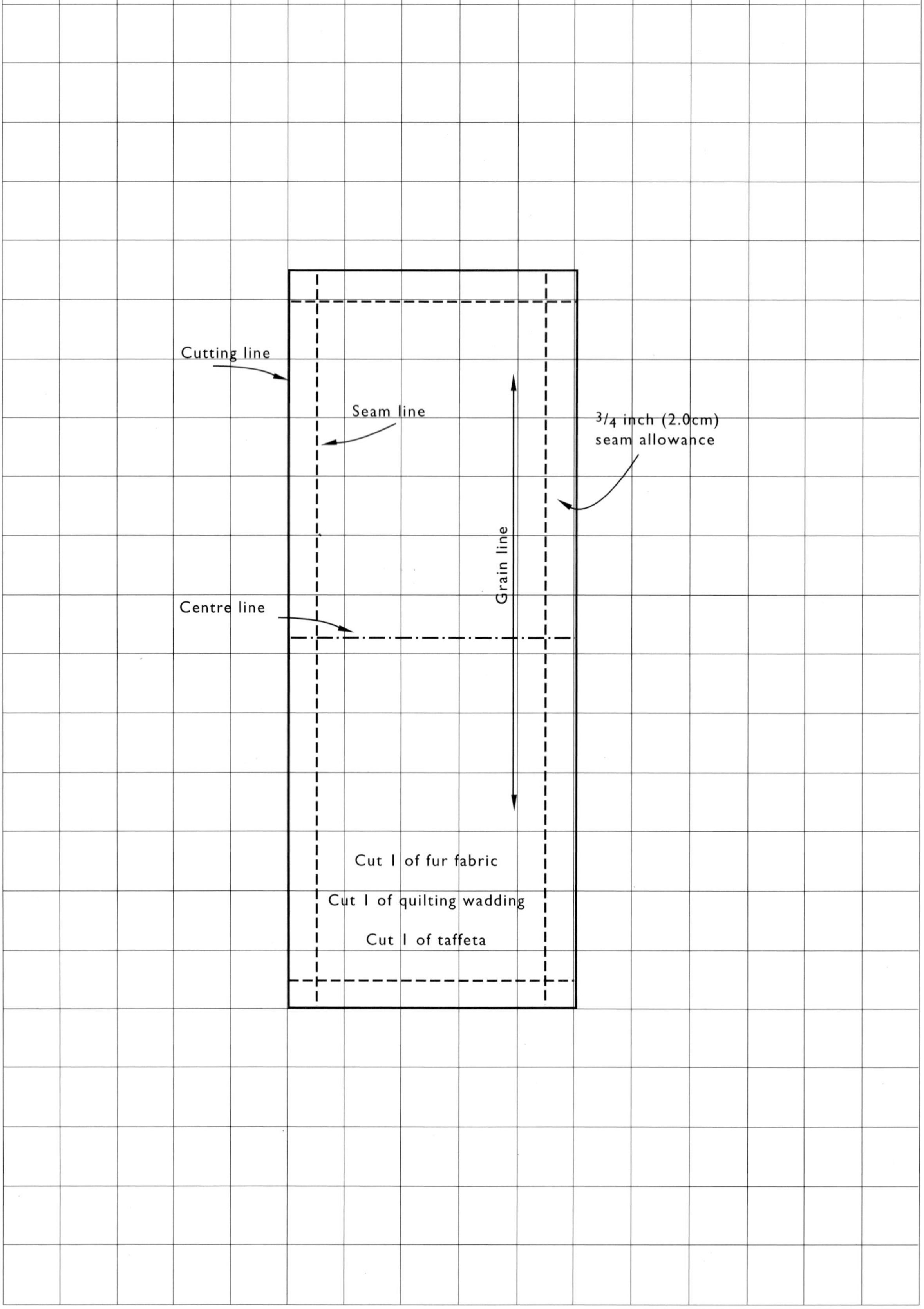

Cutting line
Seam line
3/4 inch (2.0cm) seam allowance
Grain line
Centre line
Cut 1 of fur fabric
Cut 1 of quilting wadding
Cut 1 of taffeta